THE ONE-PAN COLLEGE COOKBOOK

THE
ONE-PAN
COLLEGE
COOKBOOK

80 EASY RECIPES FOR QUICK, GOOD FOOD

MJ HONG

PHOTOGRAPHY BY DARREN MUIR

ROCKRIDGE PRESS

For general information on our other products and services or to obtain technical support, please contact our Customer Care Department within the United States at (866) 744-2665, or outside the United States at (510) 253-0500.

Rockridge Press publishes its books in a variety of electronic and print formats. Some content that appears in print may not be available in electronic books, and vice versa.

TRADEMARKS: Rockridge Press and the Rockridge Press logo are trademarks or registered trademarks of Callisto Media Inc. and/or its affiliates, in the United States and other countries, and may not be used without written permission. All other trademarks are the property of their respective owners. Rockridge Press is not associated with any product or vendor mentioned in this book.

Interior and Cover Designer: Karmen Lizzul
Art Producer: Samantha Ulban
Editor: Kelly Koester
Production Editor: Sigi Nacson
Production Manager: Martin Worthington

Photography © 2021 Darren Muir. Food Styling by Yolanda Muir.

Paperback ISBN: 978-1-63807-309-3
eBook ISBN: 978-1-63807-214-0

R0

This cookbook is dedicated to
my granddaughter, Liliana

KOREAN-INSPIRED BEEF BOWL, *page 104*

CONTENTS

**GOOEY
PIZZA DIP,**
page 40

INTRODUCTION

While college can be one of the most rewarding experiences, the lifestyle can be overwhelming and busy. College also means being on your own for meals.

If you have limited cooking experience, then it's understandable if takeout or the dining hall is your go-to for meals. You may think you don't have the time to learn a new skill or that it's difficult to cook with limited equipment, space, and budget.

This cookbook was designed to help busy college students with these cooking challenges. In addition to easy and delicious recipes all made in one pan, there are also meal planning tips and creative ideas to make the most out of ingredients and leftovers to save time and money.

I've been teaching cooking classes for the past 11 years, and my experience has inspired me to develop recipes for college students and beginner cooks.

When writing this book, the factors I considered most important for the recipes are that they be budget-friendly, have delicious flavors and be simple to make, include substitutions for dietary needs, offer options for leftovers the next day, and strike a balance between healthy and comforting.

Cooking your own meals will be less expensive, healthier, and more rewarding than getting takeout or eating in the dining hall. In addition, the recipes and techniques you learn from this book will set a foundation to build upon after college or as you gain access to more cooking equipment or space.

I hope you have fun with cooking on your college journey.

WEEKLY PLANS

	Wednesday	Thursday	Friday
...00am		Classes all day ✳ ⟵⟶ ✳	
	Lecture - 3:15pm		

Shopping List:
Chicken thighs
Garlic
Spinach
Mushrooms
Onions
Oregano

Weekend Plans:
Study:

SKILLET
CHOCOLATE
CHIP
COOKIES,
page 120

CHAPTER 1

Cooking through College with Just One Pan

This chapter covers everything you need to start cooking using just one pan. With information on the types of pan to use, essential kitchen and pantry items, as well as grocery shopping tips and guidelines for the recipes, you'll be ready and confident to start cooking easy, delicious meals in no time.

One Pan Is All You Need

A skillet is the only pan you need for this book. It's a simple but essential kitchen tool for making breakfast, snacks, and complete meals like pastas, burgers, sandwiches, stir-fries, and even desserts.

The easy-to-follow recipes in this book will show all the different dishes you can whip up no matter your cooking experience. One-pan cooking is perfect for college cooks for many reasons in addition to versatility:

→ **Quick cooking.** Cooking all the ingredients in one pan means your food will be ready in less time than it takes to have takeout delivered.

→ **Complete meals.** You can cook a complete meal in one pan without struggling with multiple pots and pans or needing time management skills to have everything ready at the same time.

→ **Reheating leftovers.** It's easy to reheat leftovers in a skillet without a microwave. It's also great for reheating items that tend to get soggy in a microwave, like pizza.

→ **Retaining flavor.** When searing (browning) meat in a pan, a crust develops that provides more flavor and seals in the juices. Plus, the leftover bits from browning add a caramelized flavor to the other ingredients in the pan.

→ **Saving space.** With just one pan, you don't need much storage or cooking space.

→ **Faster cleanup.** One pan means fewer dishes and less mess, which makes cleanup a breeze.

HAVE FUN COOKING FOR ONE

Cooking can be fun and stress-free once you learn the basics of how the process comes together. You'll have fun experimenting with new dishes and flavors and will be impressing your friends in no time.

Cooking for one also means you can cook exactly what you want, when you want. You have the freedom to add your favorite ingredients and spices and cook when your schedule allows. You can even dance to your favorite music while cooking!

Use the grocery shopping tips (see Shopping Like a Genius, page 16), and you'll be surprised by how easy it is to shop for only what you need while enjoying the process and also saving money.

When you have a busy schedule with exams or projects, make extra servings at the beginning of the week so you can focus on your studies instead of deciding what's for dinner or spending money on takeout. During those extra-busy times, cook the recipes with the "One and Done" label for easy, complete meals.

All about Pans

When selecting a pan, there are various options to consider, including type, size, material, and cost. They all perform the same basic functions of sautéing, stir-frying, pan-frying, griddling, and simmering.

The best pans for one-pan cooking are nonstick, stainless steel, or electric skillets. While you don't need to purchase the top-of-the-line models or brands, there are different factors to consider based on where you live and your personal preference. With proper care, these pans can last for years.

Nonstick Pan

Nonstick pans are made of aluminum with a coating of Teflon that prevents food from sticking to the pan and acts as a barrier between the food and the aluminum. You can tell if it's a nonstick pan by the dark gray, smooth, and shiny surface.

This type of pan works well for beginner cooks because food doesn't stick to the pan. It's also healthier since you need little to no oil for cooking, and cleanup is easy with no scrubbing involved. Popular nonstick pan brands for beginners are Calphalon, T-fal, and All-Clad.

Proper care is a must. It's important that you not use a metal utensil for cooking or scrub with an abrasive sponge while cleaning. To clean, you need only a soft sponge and soap to gently wash the pan. If you see any chipping or any of the coating wearing off on the surface, you'll need to replace the pan.

While you can generally pan-fry foods over medium heat, you cannot use very high heat to sear meats or deep-fry in a nonstick pan. Cooking on very high heat causes the pan to overheat, which causes the Teflon to release toxic fumes. You also can't preheat an empty pan for the same overheating issue. As long as you don't cook at extremely high heat, you won't have any problems.

Stainless Steel Skillet

Stainless steel skillets are more durable than nonstick pans, they can cook at high heat, and their surface doesn't wear off or chip because it's uncoated. With proper care, they can last years.

The drawback to using this pan is food sticking. You must preheat the pan with oil before adding food. While these pans are great for searing meats or deep-frying, you'll need to add enough oil or butter to create a nonstick surface when cooking delicate foods, such as fish or eggs, to prevent sticking.

For cleaning, it's important to dry the pan immediately after washing to avoid calcium buildup and water spots left on the pan. If you don't properly wash the pan, especially after cooking at high heat, you will also have stains left on the pan that will not come off, no matter how much you scrub.

With high heat, you may also see a rainbow color change to the pan. Known as "heat tint," this is normal and has nothing to do with the quality of the pan, and it's completely safe to continue using it. The easiest way to remove the rainbow stain is to cover the bottom of the pan with white vinegar, let sit for 10 minutes, then rinse the pan with water.

Electric Skillet

Electric skillets are great for college cooking if you don't have a stovetop or portable burner. The electric skillet cooks food evenly by maintaining the temperature you preset. Electric skillets are portable, so you can take the skillet to cook at a gathering or to keep food warm (you'll need an outlet). If you do this, make sure the skillet has a lid with a locking mechanism, so food doesn't spill during transport.

Electric skillets come in a variety of sizes and shapes. The rectangle shape provides more cooking surface than a round shape for items like burgers and sandwiches. If you plan to deep-fry, check that the temperature can reach 450°F. Electric skillets are available in both nonstick and stainless steel, and you should follow the proper care and cleaning instructions as provided on pages 4 and 5.

For your safety, never leave an electric skillet unattended while in use or still hot, and be sure to unplug it from the wall when not in use to prevent fire hazards. To clean, wait until the skillet is cool, and don't submerge it entirely in water.

A NOTE ON CAST IRON

Cast-iron skillets are beloved by many home cooks—they are durable and difficult to ruin, so they can be used for generations. Many take pride in using ones that have been handed down to them.

A cast-iron skillet can cook at high heat, which is perfect for searing meats, and it keeps food warm longer than other pans. It can also go from stovetop to oven to table for serving.

When you buy a new cast-iron skillet, there's a layer of oil on the surface called "seasoning." This layer is what keeps food from sticking to the pan. Each time you use it, you need to reseason the pan to maintain the nonstick surface.

Use a little soap and water to clean a new skillet to remove dirt or residue. After that, don't use soap to clean the pan after cooking because it will remove the seasoning.

To properly clean after each use, scrub off any food with a brush or sponge and run the pan under hot water, if needed. Heat over low heat to remove all moisture and prevent any rust. Add some oil and, using a paper towel, rub over the surface to create a layer of seasoning.

While a cast-iron skillet can be used for recipes in this book, it is not required.

Bringing the Heat

The two best types of heat sources for cooking are portable electric hot plates and stoves. When using any heat source, it's important to dry the food, such as meat or vegetables, before adding to hot oil as the moisture can cause the oil to splatter.

Hot Plates

Hot plates are portable, ready-to-use stoves for small spaces without a kitchen, like a dorm. Single or double burners are available, but the following information relates to single burners only.

When searching for hot plates, look for those that are energy efficient, have a cool-to-touch base, have adjustable temperature controls, heat food evenly, and are easy to clean and store.

There are some safety tips to keep in mind. First, make sure the pan is completely dry before placing it on the hot plate, as the moisture can cause damage. Next, wipe down the surface after each use to remove any food or oil. Finally, don't use the hot plate if you see a crack or damage on any component, and unplug it when not in use. There are two types of heating elements available: electric and induction. Read some reviews before selecting a hot plate, and see the manufacturer's instructions for a complete list of safety tips before using.

Electric hot plates come with an exposed coil, an integrated coil with a smooth surface, or a cast-iron surface. Read about the pros and cons of each type before selecting.

Induction hot plates use electromagnetic heat, which only reacts with a special magnetic bottom pan. While induction hot plates cook faster, they can be more expensive.

Stoves

If you have access to a kitchen, the stove will be powered by either gas or electric. Stoves have different size burners used for different size pans. Don't use a small pan on a large burner, as you can burn your food, and vice versa—don't use a big pan on a small burner, as food won't cook efficiently.

With gas stoves, you have better control over the temperature because you can instantly change the heat with a turn of the knob and can see the level of heat by looking at the flame. Gas stoves produce heat immediately once you turn on the flame, so food cooks quickly. This is very useful when stir-frying or searing meats to prevent overcooking. When the heat is turned off, the cooking stops immediately, so there's no worry of overcooking.

Electric stoves are slower to respond with temperature change, which may delay how quickly your food cooks, or it can lead to overcooking as the burner remains hot for a few minutes.

With electric stoves, it can be difficult to tell if the stove is on or off, so take care not to burn yourself. Many stove surfaces are either glass or ceramic, so take extra care to not drop the pan on the surface as it can cause damage. Cleaning electric stoves with a glass or ceramic surface is easier than cleaning gas stoves because there's only one flat surface to take care of.

5 PAN-TASTIC KITCHEN HACKS

A skillet has many functions. Here are a few unconventional uses:

1. **SANDWICH PRESS:** In a pan, heat 1 tablespoon oil or butter over medium heat. Place the sandwich in the center and press down with a lid, or place a plate on top of the sandwich and press down with a lid or spatula. Cook on both sides until browned.

2. **REHEAT PIZZA:** Forget soggy crust! For a crispy crust, place the pizza in the pan and cover it with a lid or aluminum foil. Cook over medium-low heat for 5 minutes, or until the bottom is crispy.

3. **TOFU PRESS:** The trick to getting crispy tofu is to remove any excess liquid before cooking. Lay a paper towel on a plate, add the tofu, cover with another paper towel, and sit the skillet on top for about 30 minutes to press out excess liquid.

4. **MEAT POUNDER:** If your meat is too thick, place it in a zip-top plastic bag or between sheets of plastic wrap. Holding the handle of the pan, use the bottom of the skillet to pound the meat. Now you have a thinner piece of meat you can cut up into smaller pieces.

5. **NUTCRACKER:** Holding the handle, use the bottom of the pan to crack open the shells of nuts like walnuts and macadamias. You can also then toast the nuts by placing them in a dry pan on medium-high heat for few minutes.

Kitchen Helpers

A few essential cooking tools and pantry and fridge ingredients will be helpful to make the recipes in this book. The pan pals are inexpensive and can be found at big-box stores like Walmart or Target, or online. The pantry and fridge items are needed for most of the recipes in this book. If something doesn't meet your dietary needs, you can substitute with alternate versions that do.

Pan Pals

These are a few kitchen tools that will be helpful for your one-pan cooking.

→ **Can opener:** Look for one with the added feature of a bottle opener.

→ **Kitchen scissors:** In addition to opening containers, scissors can be used to cut herbs, meat, bacon, bread, pizza, or vegetables. With scissors, you don't need a cutting board. Just make sure you use scissors made for food and not all-purpose scissors, as the blades are different. And don't ever use them to cut nonfood items to prevent contamination.

→ **Knife and wood or heavy-duty plastic cutting board:** A high-quality knife is ideal, but a basic one will do the job, too.

→ **Mixing bowls:** Use for mixing ingredients, or to store and serve foods such as salads, pastas, and popcorn. Choose a nonreactive kind, such as stainless steel, plastic, glass, or ceramic, as they are safer for acidic ingredients like vinegar and lemon.

→ **Sieve:** Use to strain foods, drain liquid from cans, or drain water from produce after washing.

→ **Spatula:** Use to flip foods such as sandwiches, eggs, quesadillas, or burgers. While the handle can be metal, choose one with a silicone or plastic edge to prevent scratches to your pan.

→ **Tongs:** For holding and gripping food items while searing, sautéing, grilling, and serving, tongs are another tool you should try to find with silicone or plastic ends to prevent scratching.

→ **Wooden spoon:** Use for tasks such as stirring, mixing, scraping, sautéing, and even smashing garlic cloves. A wooden spoon can be used with any type of pan because it won't scratch nonstick surfaces.

Pan(try)

Here are some essential pantry and staple items that are ideal to have on hand and are used in many of the recipes in this book.

→ **Bread:** Add some deli meat, slather on peanut butter and jelly, or make a grilled cheese or egg sandwich for a quick, easy, and satisfying meal.

→ **Broth:** Broth is often instead of water to add more flavor. To save money and space, you can use broth cubes, also called bouillon cubes.

→ **Canned beans:** These provide fiber and protein for a balanced meal. Depending on your preference, use chickpeas or black, pinto, white, or red beans.

→ **Oil:** Olive oil or coconut oil will be the most versatile for cooking. You can also use avocado oil, but it is more expensive. For frying or baking, a neutral oil such as vegetable is best.

→ **Pasta:** Many types and shapes of pasta are available today. You can easily get gluten-free pasta now, or try spiralized zucchini or butternut squash for low-carb options.

→ **Rice and quinoa:** Different types of rice include white, brown, jasmine, or basmati. Or substitute quinoa in any of the recipes here that call for rice. Both rice and quinoa are gluten-free and are frequently used as a side dish or as a base in one-pan meals.

→ **Salsa:** Not just for dipping with chips, salsa brings a ton of flavor to egg, meat, and rice dishes.

→ **Soy sauce:** An essential ingredient for Asian-style dishes. For a gluten-free option, substitute tamari or coconut aminos.

→ **Spices:** You'll be surprised how spices and dried herbs can enhance the taste of dishes. Some essential spices are salt, pepper, oregano, garlic powder, paprika, cumin, chili powder, and ground cinnamon. These are inexpensive and can be found at all major grocery stores. Buy the generic or store brand, which will be less expensive than brand-name products.

→ **Sweetener:** Brown and white sugar will work for recipes that call for an added sweetener. Other options include honey, agave syrup, and maple syrup.

→ **Tomatoes and tomato sauce:** Cans or jars of crushed tomatoes, diced tomatoes, or tomato sauce are added to one-pan pastas, chili, and casseroles. Look for those that have no added sugar and are low in sodium.

Fridge

Have some staple ingredients waiting in your fridge for healthy snack options or to make a quick meal. This is helpful, especially when you're up late studying or need something quick before class. Here are some items to stock in a fridge with limited space and that won't blow your budget.

Baby spinach: Keep a small bag in the fridge to make a salad along with any other vegetables on hand, or add a handful when making bowls, eggs, wraps, sandwiches, or pastas.

Cheese: String cheese and single-serve cheeses are great to have on hand for snacking or to grab to go. Have a package of shredded cheese available to use in tacos, eggs, sandwiches, pastas, or bowls.

Eggs: Eggs are versatile, filling, and a great source of protein. Fry them to make an egg sandwich or a quick scramble for breakfast or snack, or hard-boil them to take on-the-go.

Fruit: Have grapes, berries, apples, or other fruits available for a healthy snack or to grab and go. The classic combo of sliced apples with nut butter makes a great protein-filled snack. Drizzle some honey on top for those late-night sweet cravings.

MAXIMIZING YOUR MINI FRIDGE

Keep your mini fridge clean and efficiently stocked by consistently checking the dates of items inside and throwing out anything old or expired. For items that are expiring soon, find recipes in this book using those ingredients and make them next.

Purchase small sizes or quantities when available. After grocery shopping, remove all items from the fridge, or your section of the fridge if sharing with a roommate. Place any larger containers or heavier items on the bottom of the shelves so you can stack items on top, removing shelves, if needed. If you have water or other beverages taking up space, remove a few and use the space to store other ingredients.

If you purchased meat, especially chicken, it's very important that you don't place the chicken on top of fruit, vegetables, or open containers, as the juices can leak and contaminate other food. For meats, especially chicken, double wrap with plastic bags at the store to prevent leakage and cross-contamination when you place them in the fridge.

Greek yogurt: In addition to a healthy, high-protein breakfast or snack, plain Greek yogurt can also be used as a marinade for chicken or as a substitute for heavy or sour cream in recipes.

Vegetables: Stock your fridge with vegetables that require minimal prep and don't take up a lot of space in the fridge, such as baby carrots, snap peas, Persian (mini) cucumbers, and grape tomatoes. They're great for tossing together a quick salad, for snacking on, or to take with you as you run out the door.

Shopping Like a Genius

Before grocery shopping, the most important thing is to make a list, so you know what you're buying ahead of time. Be sure to always have a list or plan when you shop so you don't buy things you don't need. And make sure you're not hungry when you shop, or you will be tempted to buy unnecessary junk food. Here are some more tips for successful grocery shopping.

Weekly ads. Depending on the stores in your area, many will have great deals advertised with weekly sales and ads. Each week, look for specific items on sale or under promotions like "buy one, get one free," "two for one," or "50 percent off." These deals are especially helpful with meats, which can be expensive. Even items that have a special price for a certain amount, such as "buy three for $5," don't actually require you to buy that amount; the lower price still applies. Browse sale items online, then find recipes in this book using those items, and plan your meals for the week accordingly.

Discounted items. Many grocery items have a sell-by date, including meats, dairy, and produce. If the sell-by date is close, the store usually adds a sticker with discount pricing. When buying meats and produce, always look for discounted items, as they can save you a good deal of money.

Seasonal produce. Buy in-season produce to get not only the best pricing but also the best quality and taste.

Store brands. Buy the store or generic brands for the lowest pricing. These typically cost less than major brands.

Buy in bulk. For pantry or nonrefrigerated items you eat often, buy in bulk. You may not want to pay more at the time, but buying the larger size or quantity is usually cheaper and cost-efficient. Also check stores that sell pantry items such as rice, beans, and nuts in bulk—you can buy exactly what you need, which will cost less than prepackaged items. But think ahead, and don't buy something in bulk that won't fit in the fridge.

5 ONE-PAN WONDERS TO WOW YOUR FRIENDS

Once you have a few recipes under your belt, you'll soon be inviting friends over to show off your awesome new cooking skills. These "One and Done" meals are the perfect dishes to share with friends.

1. **CHICKEN AND BROCCOLI PASTA (PAGE 90):** Announce that it's pasta night, and serve this to a group with simple side salads or on its own.

2. **EASY LASAGNA (PAGE 108):** Get all the classic lasagna flavors without all the work with pasta that's cooked in the same pan as everything else.

3. **HEALTHY ORANGE CHICKEN (PAGE 95):** Enjoy a healthier version of this take-out favorite that's ready in under 20 minutes and is actually good for you. Double the recipe for a group.

4. **SHRIMP JAMBALAYA (PAGE 85):** This classic New Orleans dish is flavor-packed and perfect for sharing with others. Add your favorite meat, or make it vegetarian by omitting the shrimp and doubling the veggies.

5. **VEGETARIAN CHILI (PAGE 80):** This is both healthy and comforting—a dish everyone can enjoy and customize with their favorite toppings. Double the ingredients to make a big batch for friends.

The Recipes in This Book

The recipes in this book are easy to follow and can be prepared in dorm rooms or small kitchen spaces using a 10-inch skillet, with no other cookware required. A lid may be required for some of the recipes, but suggestions are always provided if you don't have one.

Each chapter includes a few recipes that serve one, but most of the recipes produce two servings, either for two people or to have leftovers. And occasionally a recipe yeilds enough for four people, making it perfect for sharing with friends (not to mention making great leftovers).

All of the recipes have labels to help guide you with meal planning and dietary needs: **5 or Fewer Ingredients** (not counting oil, salt, pepper, water, and optional ingredients), **20-Minute Meal** (ready in 20 minutes or less), **Cheap Eats** (recipes that cost less than $2 per serving—the price of a pizza slice), **Healthy** (recipes on the lighter side and that usually include fruit, vegetables, or a whole grain), **One and Done** (for complete meals), **Vegetarian** or **Vegan**. The recipes are a mix of light dishes and more filling comfort foods.

Each recipe also contains tips that help with things like smart shopping, ways for adjusting ingredients based on preference, as well as helpful cooking notes and ideas for changing up the recipe for variety.

Let's get cooking!

**BREAKFAST
VEGGIE
SKILLET,**
page 32

Breakfast

....

Easy Pancakes

SERVES 1 OR 2

PREP TIME: 5 minutes

COOK TIME: 10 minutes

TOTAL TIME: 15 minutes

1 cup all-purpose flour or gluten-free flour

1 teaspoon baking powder

1 to 2 tablespoons sugar

1/2 teaspoon salt

1 large egg

3/4 cup milk of choice, plus more as needed

1 tablespoon unsalted butter or olive oil

Optional toppings: syrup, honey, chocolate chips, or fruit

SUBSTITUTION: If you don't have baking powder, use 1/4 teaspoon baking soda and 1 tablespoon distilled white vinegar or lemon juice instead.

Pancakes are a hearty breakfast made with simple pantry ingredients. Make plain pancakes or add some chocolate chips, ground cinnamon, banana slices, or berries. The baking powder is what makes them light and fluffy, but if you don't have it, see Tip.

1. In a bowl, mix together the flour, baking powder, sugar, and salt.

2. Create a well in the center, crack in the egg, and whisk the egg with a fork. Pour in the milk and mix until combined. If the batter is too thick, stir in 1 to 2 tablespoons of additional milk.

3. In a pan, heat the butter over medium heat.

4. Pour about 1/4 cup of the batter into the center of the pan and cook until bubbles appear on the surface and the edges are set and brown. Flip over the pancake and cook the other side until golden brown.

5. Transfer to a plate and repeat with the remaining batter.

6. Top with syrup or your favorite toppings and serve.

French Toast

SERVES 1

PREP TIME: 5 minutes

COOK TIME: 10 minutes

TOTAL TIME: 15 minutes

¼ cup milk of choice

1 large egg

½ teaspoon vanilla extract (optional)

¼ teaspoon ground cinnamon

Pinch salt

1 tablespoon unsalted butter

2 slices bread

Optional toppings: maple syrup, honey, powdered sugar, or berries

French toast is a classic treat for breakfast or brunch. Use traditional white, cinnamon-raisin, or brioche bread to make this childhood favorite, and cook it until it is golden on the outside and light and fluffy on the inside.

1. In a bowl or a shallow dish, combine the milk, egg, vanilla (if using), cinnamon, and salt and whisk together with a fork.

2. In a pan, melt the butter over medium heat.

3. Soak both sides of the bread in the milk/egg mixture, letting any excess drip into the bowl. Transfer to the pan and cook for 3 to 4 minutes, until lightly browned on each side.

4. If desired, serve with the toppings of your choice.

SMART SHOPPING: Stale bread works best for French toast. Make this recipe when the loaf you bought is beginning to get too stale to eat fresh. If serving this recipe for a crowd, use cut-up slices of a French baguette to create smaller serving sizes.

Healthy Oatmeal with Fruit

5 OR FEWER INGREDIENTS · 20-MINUTE MEAL · CHEAP EATS · HEALTHY · ONE AND DONE · VEGAN

SERVES 1

PREP TIME: 5 minutes

COOK TIME: 5 minutes

TOTAL TIME: 10 minutes

1½ cups water

¾ cup old-fashioned
   rolled oats

Pinch salt

Pinch ground cinnamon

Toppings of choice

Oatmeal is healthy and quick to prepare, and it can be customized with toppings. Try it plain or with apples and brown sugar, dried or fresh fruit, or chopped nuts. Once you've mastered basic oatmeal, you can change it up with whatever you have on hand. Check out the tip on this page to make overnight oats.

1. In a pan, bring the water to a boil over high heat.

2. Reduce the heat to low, stir in the oats, salt, and cinnamon and cook, stirring often, for 4 to 5 minutes, until the liquid is absorbed.

3. Transfer to a bowl and eat plain or add any desired toppings.

COOKING TIP: For overnight oats, combine ½ cup of uncooked oats and ½ of cup milk in a jar or container with a lid. Top with any desired fruit or nuts (but don't mix the toppings into the oatmeal), cover, and refrigerate overnight. In the morning, stir the mixture together and serve cold.

Hard-Boiled Eggs

SERVES 1
PREP TIME: 1 minute
COOK TIME: 17 minutes
TOTAL TIME: 18 minutes

2 large eggs

Water

Make perfect hard-boiled eggs that are easy to peel and without a green ring around the yolk! Not only do hard-boiled eggs make a healthy breakfast or snack, but they are also great in sandwiches or added to salads for extra protein.

1. Place the eggs in a pan and cover them halfway with water. Cover with a lid or aluminum foil and bring to a boil over high heat. Turn off the heat and let sit, covered, for 15 minutes. (Do not open the lid during this time—the eggs will still be cooking.)

2. Carefully transfer the pan to the sink or remove the eggs with a slotted spoon or tongs and place them in a bowl. Rinse with cold running water until the eggs are cool.

3. Gently tap the shells on a hard surface and peel the shells. Store any leftover eggs in a covered container and refrigerate for up to 5 days.

COOKING TIP: Make extra eggs so you'll have them on hand for high-protein, to-go breakfasts or snacks, to make Deviled Egg Bites (page 64), or to add to the Healthy Breakfast Bowl (page 27).

Skillet Chilaquiles

20-MINUTE MEAL · ONE AND DONE

SERVES 2 TO 4

PREP TIME: 5 minutes

COOK TIME: 15 minutes

TOTAL TIME: 20 minutes

1 tablespoon olive oil

½ onion, diced

½ teaspoon salt

½ teaspoon ground black pepper

½ teaspoon ground cumin

2 garlic cloves, minced

1 (16-ounce) can red or green enchilada sauce

1½ cups cooked shredded chicken

3 cups tortilla chips (enough to fill the pan)

Optional toppings: crumbled queso fresco, sliced jalapeño peppers, diced avocado, and chopped tomatoes

Nachos for breakfast? Yes, please! This dish is a good one to enjoy with friends on the weekends. Keep it simple, make a vegetarian version, or load it up with toppings based on what you have on hand. This recipe uses shredded chicken, which you might have left over from making Rotisserie Enchiladas (page 91).

1. In a pan, heat the oil over medium heat. Add the onion and cook, stirring, for 3 minutes.

2. Add the salt, pepper, cumin, and garlic and cook, stirring often, for about 1 minute, or until fragrant.

3. Add the enchilada sauce and chicken, reduce the heat to low, and cook, stirring occasionally, for 5 minutes.

4. Stir in the tortilla chips and mix until evenly coated with the sauce and slightly soft or still crisp, depending on your preference.

5. Transfer to a plate, add the toppings (if using), and serve immediately.

COOKING TIP: To top with a fried egg, cook the egg in the pan first and set aside. Make the chilaquiles as directed, and top with the fried egg when serving.

Healthy Breakfast Bowl

20-MINUTE MEAL · HEALTHY · ONE AND DONE · VEGETARIAN

SERVES 1

PREP TIME: 5 minutes

COOK TIME: 10 minutes

TOTAL TIME: 15 minutes

1 tablespoon olive oil

1 large egg

1 cup chopped vegetables, such as bell peppers, broccoli, cauliflower, and mushrooms

Pinch salt

Pinch ground black pepper

1 cup cooked quinoa or rice

1 cup packed spinach (or any other greens)

Optional toppings: sliced avocado and chopped tomatoes

This hearty bowl is healthy and quickly made to get your nutrition when you wake up—perfect for busy mornings. By using precooked quinoa or rice, you'll have breakfast ready in 15 minutes. It's easy to customize with your favorite vegetables or ingredients. You can also add leftover Pan-Fried Chickpeas (page 45) or Smashed Potatoes (page 47). You'll be glad you did.

1. In a pan, heat the oil over medium heat. Add the egg and scramble until cooked to your liking. Set aside on a plate.

2. Add the chopped vegetables, salt, and pepper to the pan and cook, stirring, for about 3 minutes, or until tender.

3. Add the quinoa and cook, stirring, until warm throughout.

4. Add the spinach and scrambled egg and stir until the spinach is slightly wilted.

5. Transfer to a bowl. If desired, garnish with one of the toppings and eat while it's still hot.

MAKE IT FASTER: Make a double batch and store leftovers in the fridge for a quick breakfast, lunch, or snack. To heat, stir-fry in a pan over medium heat until warm.

Pasta Frittata

5 OR FEWER INGREDIENTS · 20-MINUTE MEAL · CHEAP EATS · ONE AND DONE · VEGETARIAN

SERVES 1
PREP TIME: 5 minutes
COOK TIME: 10 minutes
TOTAL TIME: 15 minutes

1 large egg

½ cup grated
   Parmesan cheese

1 cup cooked pasta
   (see Tip)

1 tablespoon olive oil

SUBSTITUTION: If you
don't have cooked pasta
available, cook 2 ounces
spaghetti or your favorite
pasta in a pan according
to the package directions.
Drain and continue with
the recipe instructions.

In this recipe, the pasta is already cooked, so the dish comes together quite quickly. This is a good place to use leftover pasta if you have it. And if you have extra veggies or greens, such as spinach leaves, feel free to add them. This tasty meal reheats well, so make extra (1 egg for every 1 cup of pasta) and save it for a quick snack, lunch, or dinner. Store it in an airtight container and refrigerate for up to 3 days.

1. In a bowl, whisk the egg and Parmesan together with a fork. Add the pasta and mix well.

2. In a pan, heat the oil over medium heat. Add the pasta mixture evenly to the pan and press down with a spatula. Cook for 4 to 5 minutes, until golden and crisp around the edges.

3. Carefully flip the frittata over with a spatula and cook the other side for 4 to 5 minutes, until golden and crisp on the second side.

4. Transfer to a plate and cut into wedges or squares. Eat while it's still hot.

Breakfast Quesadilla

SERVES 1

PREP TIME: 5 minutes

COOK TIME: 10 minutes

TOTAL TIME: 15 minutes

1 tablespoon oil or butter

2 large eggs

Salt

Ground black pepper

½ cup chopped or crumbled add-ins (optional)

½ cup shredded cheese of choice

1 large flour tortilla

MAKE IT FASTER: Make an extra quesadilla to reheat the next day. Reheat the quesadilla in 1 teaspoon oil in a pan over medium heat until the tortilla is crisp.

Quesadillas are delicious in their simplest form with tortillas and cheese but can be made even better by adding some scrambled eggs (as done here), sliced deli meats, precooked crumbled sausage, or diced vegetables like bell peppers, onions, or tomatoes. It's up to you and the contents of your fridge.

1. In a pan, heat the oil over medium heat.
2. In a bowl, beat the eggs with a fork and season with salt and pepper. (If you are adding additional ingredients like veggies or meat, add them now.)
3. Reduce the heat to medium-low, add the eggs (or egg mixture), and cook, stirring occasionally, until the eggs are cooked through.
4. Sprinkle the cheese evenly over the eggs and gently press the tortilla on top of the cheese.
5. Place a spatula under the eggs and carefully flip over the eggs and tortilla. Fold the tortilla in half.
6. Gently press with the spatula and cook on both sides until the tortilla is golden brown.
7. Cut into wedges and eat while it's still hot.

Breakfast Pizza

SERVES 1

PREP TIME: 5 minutes

COOK TIME: 5 minutes

TOTAL TIME: 10 minutes

½ cup chopped toppings (optional)

1 teaspoon olive oil (optional)

1 flour or corn tortilla

Spoonful of pizza or pasta sauce

½ cup shredded mozzarella cheese

This breakfast pizza uses a tortilla as the crust. Load it up with your favorite toppings or other ingredients that need to be used up.

1. Cook or heat any toppings in a pan with about 1 teaspoon oil until warm, set aside on a plate, then wipe out the pan with a paper towel.

2. In the pan, heat the tortilla over medium heat for about 1 minute on each side.

3. Spoon the tomato sauce on top of the tortilla and use the back of the spoon to spread it into a thin layer. Top with the heated additional ingredients (if using), then sprinkle with the mozzarella.

4. Once the bottom of the tortilla starts to get crisp, remove from the heat.

5. Cover with a lid or a sheet of aluminum foil to melt the cheese. Cut into wedges and eat while still hot.

REMIX TIP: Make this with store-bought pizza dough instead to serve more people. On a clean work surface, stretch and form the dough into a round shape, slightly smaller than the pan (depending on the size of the pan, you may only need half of the dough). In the pan, heat 1 tablespoon of oil over medium heat. Add the dough and cook for 2 minutes. Flip over and add the pizza sauce, any toppings, and shredded cheese. Cover and cook for 2 to 3 minutes, until the bottom is golden brown and the cheese is melted. Cut into wedges.

Sausage and Potato Hash

5 OR FEWER INGREDIENTS · HEALTHY · ONE AND DONE

SERVES 2

PREP TIME: 10 minutes

COOK TIME: 20 minutes

TOTAL TIME: 30 minutes

1 tablespoon olive oil

½ pound Italian sausage, casings removed

1 large or 2 small russet potatoes, peeled and cubed

½ onion, diced

2 garlic cloves, minced

1 red bell pepper, chopped

½ teaspoon salt, plus more to taste

½ teaspoon ground black pepper, plus more to taste

This comforting dish is ideal for weekend brunch when you have more time. It calls for Italian sausage, but feel free to use breakfast links, chorizo, bacon, or ham, or use something plant-based to make this vegetarian. You can also top with a fried egg or shredded cheese.

1. In a pan, heat the oil over medium heat. Add the sausage and cook, using a wooden spoon to break up the meat, for about 3 minutes, or until no longer pink.

2. Stir in the potatoes, cover with a lid or aluminum foil, and cook, stirring a couple of times, for 6 minutes.

3. Add the onion, garlic, bell pepper, salt, and black pepper and sauté for about 5 minutes, or until the potatoes are tender. Taste and add more salt and pepper, if desired.

4. Transfer to plates and serve hot.

MAKE IT FASTER: This dish is easy to reheat in the pan, so make a double batch, store half in an airtight container in the fridge, and you'll have breakfast on hand for busy mornings. To serve as lunch or dinner, sauté some additional vegetables or add cooked rice or quinoa when reheating.

Breakfast Veggie Skillet

5 OR FEWER INGREDIENTS · 20-MINUTE MEAL · HEALTHY · ONE AND DONE · VEGETARIAN

SERVES 2
PREP TIME: 5 minutes
COOK TIME: 10 minutes
TOTAL TIME: 15 minutes

1 tablespoon olive oil

2 cups chopped vegetables, such as bell peppers, broccoli, or mushrooms

1 teaspoon dried oregano

½ teaspoon salt

½ teaspoon ground black pepper

2 garlic cloves, minced

2 handfuls baby spinach or baby kale

2 large eggs

Here's another recipe that's perfect for using up veggies you have on hand. Make a double batch to have lunch or dinner ready to reheat in the pan, or for a heartier option, add cooked rice or quinoa.

1. In a pan, heat the oil over medium heat. Add the chopped vegetables, oregano, salt, and pepper and cook for about 2 minutes, or until the vegetables are soft and tender.

2. Add the garlic and spinach and cook, stirring constantly, for about 30 seconds.

3. Using a spatula or a wooden spoon, create two wells in the veggie mixture and break 1 egg into each one. Cover with a lid or aluminum foil and cook for 5 to 6 minutes, until the eggs are cooked soft or firm to your liking.

4. Transfer to plates and serve immediately.

SMART SHOPPING: Most stores have fresh vegetable medleys in a bag in the produce section, ready for stir-frying. Use half the bag for this dish and the other half for the Teriyaki Chicken and Vegetable Stir-Fry (page 94).

Simple Shakshuka

HEALTHY · ONE AND DONE · VEGETARIAN

SERVES 2

PREP TIME: 10 minutes

COOK TIME: 20 minutes

TOTAL TIME: 30 minutes

1 tablespoon olive oil

1 onion, diced

1 bell pepper (any color), chopped

2 garlic cloves, minced

1 teaspoon ground cumin

1 teaspoon paprika

1 teaspoon salt

½ teaspoon ground black pepper

1 (28-ounce) can crushed tomatoes

2 large eggs

Optional toppings: chopped fresh cilantro or parsley, and crumbled feta cheese

Bread, for serving

Pronounced "shack-shoe-kah," this tomato-based Middle Eastern and North African dish is packed with flavor and perfect for sharing with friends. Add some red pepper flakes or cayenne pepper for a little spice.

1. In a pan, heat the oil over medium heat. Add the onion and bell pepper and cook, stirring, for 3 minutes.

2. Add the garlic, cumin, paprika, salt, and black pepper and cook, stirring, for about 1 minute. Reduce the heat to low, add the crushed tomatoes, and cook, stirring, for about 5 minutes.

3. Using a spatula or wooden spoon, create two wells in the mixture and crack 1 egg into each one. Cover with a lid or aluminum foil and cook for 5 to 6 minutes, until the eggs are cooked to your liking.

4. Serve right out of the pan or transfer to a serving plate. If desired, garnish with cilantro, parsley, or feta cheese. Serve with bread to soak up the sauce.

MAKE IT FASTER: Make this a day ahead. Cook the tomato mixture (through step 2) and let cool completely. Cover and refrigerate. When ready to serve, reheat over low heat for about 3 minutes, then continue with adding the eggs and cooking as directed.

GOOEY PIZZA DIP,
page 40

Snacks and Small Bites

Healthy Protein Bites

5 OR FEWER INGREDIENTS · HEALTHY · ONE AND DONE · VEGETARIAN

MAKES 12 BITES

PREP TIME: 5 minutes, plus 1 hour to chill

COOK TIME: 2 minutes

TOTAL TIME: 1 hour, 7 minutes

½ cup nut butter of choice

3 tablespoons unsweetened almond or coconut milk

3 tablespoons honey

1 cup old-fashioned rolled oats

¼ cup unflavored protein powder

Optional add-ins: ¼ cup chocolate chips, shredded coconut, and chopped dried fruit

This protein-packed snack gives you energy between classes or before a workout. Not only will you save money, but you'll be in control of the ingredients, which makes these bites healthier than store-bought bars. The best thing about this recipe is that it's versatile. Omit the protein powder, use regular milk, add ¼ cup of flaxseed, or add 1 tablespoon of cocoa powder. You choose!

1. In a pan, heat the nut butter, milk, and honey over medium-low heat and stir until combined and smooth. Turn off the heat.

2. Stir in the oats, protein powder, and any additional ingredients you like and mix until combined.

3. Transfer to a bowl, cover with plastic wrap, and chill in the refrigerator for about 1 hour until the mixture is firm. Roll the mixture into 12 bite-size balls.

4. Eat them right away or store the bites in a covered container in the fridge for up to 5 days.

REMIX TIP: Once chilled, you can also form the mixture into bars and wrap each bar individually in plastic wrap. Store in the fridge for easy grab-and-go.

Pan-Fried Plantains

5 OR FEWER INGREDIENTS · 20-MINUTE MEAL · CHEAP EATS · HEALTHY · VEGAN

SERVES 1

PREP TIME: 5 minutes

COOK TIME: 10 minutes

TOTAL TIME: 15 minutes

2 tablespoons olive oil

2 ripe brown plantains, peeled and cut on the diagonal into slices ¼ inch thick

Salt

You only need oil, plantains, and salt to make fried plantains. Crispy, salty, and sweet all in one bite, these are so addictive you'll want to make more than one batch.

1. In a pan, heat the oil over medium-high heat. Place the plantains in the pan in a single layer and fry for 3 to 4 minutes, until browned. Flip them over and brown the other side.

2. Transfer to a plate lined with paper towels and sprinkle with salt to taste.

3. Serve hot.

COOKING TIP: If you can only get green, unripe plantains (which have thicker skin and are harder to peel), they will require an extra step of refrying. To prepare, cut off both ends of the plantain, then carefully run a knife along the peel seam from one end to the other to cut through the skin, but without cutting into the flesh. Repeat the process with 1 or 2 more seams, then carefully peel off the skin in segments. Cut and fry the plantains as directed and transfer to a plate. Using the bottom of a glass, smash the plantains flat. Add 1 tablespoon oil to the pan and fry again over medium-high heat for 2 to 3 minutes for an even crispier texture.

Shishito Peppers with Soy-Garlic Sauce

20-MINUTE MEAL · CHEAP EATS · HEALTHY · VEGAN

SERVES 1

PREP TIME: 5 minutes
COOK TIME: 10 minutes
TOTAL TIME: 15 minutes

FOR THE PEPPERS

1 tablespoon olive oil
1 cup shishito peppers
Juice of ½ lime
Salt

FOR THE SOY-GARLIC SAUCE

1 tablespoon soy sauce
1 garlic clove, minced
1 teaspoon light
  brown sugar
Juice of ½ lime

MAKE IT FASTER: Omit the sauce and just add the lime juice and salt to the pan in step 4.

This addictive snack will become one of your favorites. Shishito peppers can be found in Asian markets and most major grocery stores. They are usually mild but don't be surprised if you bite into one that's spicy—one in every ten shishito peppers can be spicy!

TO MAKE THE PEPPERS

1. In a pan, heat the oil over medium-high heat. Add the peppers and cook, turning often until they start to blister in some places.

2. Add the lime juice and a sprinkle of salt and toss until combined.

TO MAKE THE SOY-GARLIC SAUCE

3. In a small bowl, mix together the soy sauce, garlic, brown sugar, and lime juice.

4. Add the sauce to the pan and toss with the peppers. Reduce the heat to low and cook for about 5 minutes, or until the peppers are tender.

5. Eat while they're still hot.

Cheeseburger Sliders

MAKES 4 SLIDERS

PREP TIME: 10 minutes

COOK TIME: 10 minutes

TOTAL TIME: 20 minutes

½ **pound ground beef**

1 **teaspoon salt**

1 **teaspoon ground black pepper**

1 **teaspoon garlic powder**

1 **tablespoon olive oil**

4 **slices cheddar cheese**

4 **slider buns, dinner rolls, or Hawaiian rolls**

Burger toppings (optional)

REMIX TIP: Substitute ground turkey or chicken for the ground beef. For the cheese, use sliced pepper Jack for an extra kick, or top with shredded cheese instead of sliced.

Sliders are quick and easy, and leftovers can also be reheated in the pan. Their smaller size makes them easier to eat, and they are great snacks, too. Want them low-carb? Use fresh lettuce as wraps instead of buns.

1. In a bowl, combine the ground beef, salt, pepper, and garlic powder and gently mix together with your hands or a fork until just combined.

2. Divide the meat into four portions, form into balls, and flatten them with the palms of your hands to make patties.

3. In a pan, heat the oil over medium-high heat. Add the patties to the pan and cook for 2 to 5 minutes, until browned on the first side.

4. Flip the sliders over and place a cheese slice on each one. Cover with a lid or aluminum foil and cook to your desired doneness: 2 to 3 minutes for rare, 3 to 4 minutes for medium, or 4 to 5 minutes for well-done.

5. Place the patties on buns, add any desired toppings, and serve hot.

Gooey Pizza Dip

SERVES 2 TO 4

PREP TIME: 5 minutes

COOK TIME: 10 minutes

TOTAL TIME: 15 minutes

1 (8-ounce) package cream cheese, at room temperature

1 cup shredded mozzarella cheese, plus more for topping

1 teaspoon garlic powder

2 cups pizza sauce, marinara, or tomato sauce

Optional add-ins (see Tip)

Sliced bread or baguette, for dipping

Your favorite pizza toppings all in one dip! This version is vegetarian, but if you'd like, you can add some pepperoni slices or make it "supreme" with leftover diced cooked meats like ham or crumbled sausage and chopped veggies like bell peppers, onion, and tomatoes. Grab some crusty bread and dig in!

1. In a bowl, mix together the cream cheese, mozzarella, and garlic powder.

2. Evenly spread the cream cheese mixture in the pan.

3. Spoon the sauce over the cheese and top with additional mozzarella, if desired. (If you're including any optional ingredients, add them now.)

4. Cover with a lid or aluminum foil and simmer over low heat for 8 to 10 minutes, until bubbling.

5. Serve right out of the pan with bread for dipping.

COOKING TIP: If you're adding any meats that need cooking, do that in the pan first. Set aside, then add the cream cheese mixture as directed.

Leftover Rice Cakes

5 OR FEWER INGREDIENTS · 20-MINUTE MEAL · CHEAP EATS · ONE AND DONE · VEGETARIAN

SERVES 1

PREP TIME: 5 minutes

COOK TIME: 10 minutes

TOTAL TIME: 15 minutes

1 cup cooked rice

1 large egg

¼ cup grated Parmesan cheese (optional)

Pinch salt

Pinch ground black pepper

1 tablespoon olive oil

Crispy and hearty, these tasty little snacks are made using cooked rice. Make a double batch of these cakes to serve as a side dish or to have on hand for when you're hungry during the week. To reheat, heat 1 tablespoon of oil in a pan and cook the rice cakes over medium heat until warm.

1. In a bowl, mix together the rice, egg, Parmesan (if using), salt, and pepper.

2. In a pan, heat the oil over medium heat. Using your hands, form the rice mixture into 2 or 3 patties, depending on the desired size of the cakes.

3. Place the patties in the pan and flatten with a spatula. Cook for 3 to 4 minutes, until golden brown. Flip and cook another 3 to 4 minutes, until the other side is golden brown.

4. Transfer to a plate and enjoy immediately.

REMIX TIP: For Asian-inspired rice cakes, omit the Parmesan cheese and add 1 teaspoon of sesame oil and some chopped scallions to the rice mixture. Make a dipping sauce by mixing together 1 minced garlic clove, 1 tablespoon of soy sauce, 1 teaspoon of sesame oil, and 1 teaspoon of brown sugar.

Low-Carb Cheesy Taco

5 OR FEWER INGREDIENTS · 20-MINUTE MEAL · CHEAP EATS · ONE AND DONE · VEGETARIAN

SERVES 1

PREP TIME: 2 minutes

COOK TIME: 5 minutes

TOTAL TIME: 7 minutes

1 tablespoon unsalted butter or olive oil

½ cup shredded cheddar or cheese of choice

1 large egg

Pinch salt

Pinch ground black pepper

Who said eggs are only for breakfast? This low-carb taco is cheesy, delicious, and super easy to make using minimal ingredients. After you make one, you'll quickly be craving another!

1. Line a plate with paper towels.

2. In a pan, heat the butter over medium-low heat. Sprinkle the cheese evenly onto the center of the pan and shape it into a round using a spatula.

3. Crack the egg into the center of the cheese (if the egg starts to slide off the cheese, use your spatula to move the egg back onto the cheese). Reduce the heat to low, cover with a lid or aluminum foil, and cook for 1 minute, or until the egg white is set and the cheese browned.

4. Using a spatula, lift one side of the cheese and fold it over in half. Flip the folded cheese taco over and cook for about 10 more seconds to cook the egg yolk slightly.

5. Transfer to the paper towels to absorb any excess oil. Serve warm.

COOKING TIP: Make sure you don't cook on high heat—the cheese will burn quickly.

Spicy Vegan Lettuce Wraps

20-MINUTE MEAL · HEALTHY · ONE AND DONE · VEGAN

SERVES 2

PREP TIME: 10 minutes

COOK TIME: 10 minutes

TOTAL TIME: 20 minutes

7 ounces (half a 14-ounce package) firm or extra-firm tofu

2 tablespoons tamari or coconut aminos

1 tablespoon sriracha or other hot chili sauce

1 teaspoon sesame oil

1 teaspoon light brown or granulated sugar

1 tablespoon olive oil

2 garlic cloves, minced

½ teaspoon minced fresh ginger

1 cup sliced mushrooms

1 carrot, grated

6 romaine or iceberg lettuce leaves

Chopped scallion or fresh cilantro, for garnish

These lettuce wraps are low-carb and vegan. Even if you don't like tofu, give it a try—you might be surprised. The filling can be stored in an airtight container and refrigerated for up to 5 days. You can use soy sauce instead of tamari, but it won't be vegan.

1. Press the tofu between paper towels to remove any excess liquid. Let sit.

2. In a small bowl, mix together the tamari, sriracha, sesame oil, and brown sugar. Set aside.

3. In a pan, heat the olive oil over medium heat. Add the garlic and ginger and cook, stirring, for 30 seconds. Add the tofu and, using a wooden spoon, break it up into small pieces. Cook, stirring often, for 3 minutes.

4. Add the mushrooms and carrot and stir-fry for 3 minutes.

5. Pour in the sauce and continue to stir-fry for about 1 minute, until the vegetables are tender and everything is well coated with the sauce.

6. Spoon into individual lettuce leaves, top with scallion or cilantro, and serve hot.

COOKING TIP: Save the other half of the tofu package for the Healthy Buddha Bowls (page 79).

BLT Bites

SERVES 2

PREP TIME: 5 minutes

COOK TIME: 5 minutes

TOTAL TIME: 10 minutes

2 slices bacon or
turkey bacon

2 iceberg or romaine
lettuce leaves

2 tablespoons mayonnaise
or ranch dressing

1 Roma (plum) tomato,
cut into slices about
¼ inch thick

Pinch salt (optional)

This healthier, low-carb version of the classic BLT has all the flavors to satisfy your cravings. To make it even quicker to assemble, precook the bacon and prep the vegetables, then store them in the fridge. When ready to serve, assemble as directed just before eating (the tomato and mayo can make the other ingredients soggy if the dish sits too long assembled).

1. Line a plate with paper towels.

2. In a pan, cook the bacon over medium heat until crisp to your liking. Drain on the paper towels and cut or break into three to four equal pieces.

3. Lay the lettuce in a single layer on a plate. Spread the mayo on top of the lettuce. Top with sliced tomato and salt (if using). Top with the bacon and wrap together.

4. Serve immediately.

REMIX TIP: To serve with bread, use leftover slider buns or Hawaiian rolls from the Cheeseburger Sliders (page 39). Another option is to use a bell pepper cut in half and seeded instead of the lettuce.

Pan-Fried Chickpeas

5 OR FEWER INGREDIENTS · CHEAP EATS · HEALTHY · VEGAN

SERVES 1 OR 2

PREP TIME: 5 minutes

COOK TIME: 20 minutes

TOTAL TIME: 25 minutes

1 (15-ounce) can chickpeas, drained and rinsed

1 tablespoon olive oil

Salt

Ground black pepper (optional)

Your favorite spice blend (optional)

Crunchy, salty, and a healthier alternative to potato chips, this will become one of your new favorite snacks. Alter the flavors by adding your favorite spices, such as curry powder. Warning, you'll want to make more than one batch!

1. Pat the chickpeas completely dry with a paper towel.

2. In a pan, heat the oil over medium heat. Add the chickpeas and cook for about 15 minutes, stirring often, until golden brown and crispy.

3. Season with salt, pepper (if using), and your favorite spice blend (if using) and toss to coat.

4. Transfer to a plate lined with paper towels to absorb excess oil. Eat warm or at room temperature.

COOKING TIP: Make an extra batch and store in an airtight container for up to 2 days. Re-toast them in a dry pan. They also taste great in the Healthy Breakfast Bowl (page 27).

Stovetop Popcorn

5 OR FEWER INGREDIENTS · 20-MINUTE MEAL · CHEAP EATS · HEALTHY · VEGAN

SERVES 2 TO 4
PREP TIME: 2 minutes
COOK TIME: 10 minutes
TOTAL TIME: 12 minutes

2 tablespoons vegetable oil

⅓ cup popcorn kernels

Salt or seasoning blend

1 tablespoon unsalted
   butter or vegan butter

REMIX TIP: Sprinkle with grated Parmesan cheese or nutritional yeast for a cheesy flavor or with red pepper flakes or cayenne pepper for a punch of spice.

Stovetop popcorn is one of the easiest and cheapest snacks to make. The trick to cooking it perfectly on the stove without burning it is to know when the oil temperature is hot enough to add the kernels.

1. In a pan, heat the oil over medium heat for about 2 minutes. Add 2 or 3 kernels and wait for them to pop. Using tongs, remove the popped kernels from the pan.

2. Add the remaining popcorn kernels, cover with a lid or aluminum foil, and shake the pan back and forth to evenly distribute the kernels in the oil.

3. After a few minutes, the kernels will start to pop. Shake the pan again. Once the popping starts to slow down and comes to a stop, turn off the heat and leave the pan covered for about 20 seconds to make sure all the kernels are popped.

4. Pour the popcorn into a bowl and season with salt to taste or any other desired seasonings.

5. Add the butter to the pan to melt and drizzle it over the popcorn. Toss until combined and serve.

Smashed Potatoes

SERVES 2 TO 4

PREP TIME: 5 minutes

COOK TIME: 20 minutes

TOTAL TIME: 25 minutes

1 pound baby potatoes

1 teaspoon salt

1 tablespoon olive oil
 or butter

2 garlic cloves, minced
 (optional)

Salt

Ground black pepper

MAKE IT FASTER: Boil the potatoes ahead of time, drain, cool completely, and store in an airtight container in the fridge for up to 4 days. When ready to eat, pan-fry as directed for a quick snack or side dish.

Crispy on the outside and soft on the inside, these yummy potatoes make a delicious and hearty snack or side dish. Using baby potatoes instead of larger spuds reduces the cooking time by half. Add some grated Parmesan cheese, your favorite spices, or chopped fresh parsley to amp up the flavors.

1. In a pan, combine the potatoes, salt, and enough water to cover the potatoes. Bring to a boil over high heat. Reduce the heat to low and simmer for 12 to 15 minutes, until the potatoes are fork-tender.

2. Drain off the water and return the potatoes to the pan. Add the oil and garlic (if using) and cook, stirring, for about 30 seconds. Smash the potatoes with a spatula, potato masher, or the bottom of a cup.

3. Increase the heat to medium and cook for about 4 minutes, flipping over halfway, until the potatoes are golden brown.

4. Season with salt and pepper to taste and serve.

**THAI-INSPIRED
LETTUCE
WRAPS,**
page 60

CHAPTER 4

Burgers, Sandwiches, and Other Handhelds

Caramelized Onion–Stuffed Burgers

MAKES 2 BURGERS

PREP TIME: 5 minutes

COOK TIME: 15 minutes

TOTAL TIME: 20 minutes

1 tablespoon olive oil

½ onion, chopped or thinly sliced

2 tablespoons balsamic vinegar

1 tablespoon light brown sugar

½ teaspoon salt, plus more for seasoning

½ teaspoon ground black pepper, plus more for seasoning

½ pound ground beef (80% to 85% lean) or chicken

Making burgers in your skillet is really easy and takes only 20 minutes. Cooking the onions with balsamic vinegar and brown sugar caramelizes them quickly, and they taste incredible. You can also stuff the burgers with blue cheese or Gorgonzola cheese along with the onions for a twist on the traditional cheddar. For the juiciest burger, look for 80 percent to 85 percent lean for the ground beef; 90 percent lean may be too dry.

1. In a pan, heat the oil over medium-high heat. Add the onion and cook, stirring often, for 2 minutes. Add the balsamic vinegar, brown sugar, salt, and pepper and continue to cook, stirring often, for 3 minutes.

2. Divide the beef in half and, using your hands, gently flatten into two round patties. Place a spoonful of onions in the center of each patty and re-form it into a round flat patty with the onions enclosed. Transfer the remaining onions to a plate and set aside for the topping.

2 slices cheese of choice (optional)

2 hamburger buns

Optional toppings: sliced tomato and onion, lettuce, pickles, ketchup, and mustard

3. Sprinkle the patties with a pinch each of salt and pepper. Create a dimple by pressing your fingertip in the center of each patty. (This prevents the meat from doming in the middle during cooking.)

4. Heat the pan (no need to wipe it out) over medium-high heat. Add the patties and cook to your desired doneness, 3 minutes on each side for medium-rare, 4 minutes on each side for medium, 5 minutes on each side for well done. If making cheeseburgers, top each burger with a slice of cheese after the first flip.

5. Transfer to the buns. Top with the remaining caramelized onions and any of the toppings (if using), and serve.

COOKING TIP: To toast the buns, before caramelizing the onions, heat 1 teaspoon of butter or oil in the pan over medium heat. Place the buns, cut-side down, in the pan and toast until golden brown. Transfer to a plate and continue to make the onions and burgers as directed.

Cheeseburger Pitas

20-MINUTE MEAL · ONE AND DONE

MAKES 2 BURGERS

PREP TIME: 5 minutes

COOK TIME: 10 minutes

TOTAL TIME: 15 minutes

Try this spin on the classic cheeseburger. Don't have pita bread? Use a tortilla or make a lettuce wrap. To save time, make a double batch of the tzatziki sauce and use for the Greek Pita Wraps (page 56).

FOR THE TZATZIKI SAUCE

½ cup plain Greek yogurt

1 Persian cucumber, cut into small cubes

1 tablespoon freshly squeezed lemon juice

Pinch salt

Pinch ground black pepper

FOR THE CHEESE-BURGER FILLING

1 tablespoon olive oil

½ pound ground beef or chicken

½ teaspoon salt

½ teaspoon ground black pepper

½ teaspoon garlic powder

1 cup shredded cheddar cheese

2 pitas, for serving

Optional toppings: lettuce and sliced tomato

TO MAKE THE TZATZIKI SAUCE

1. In a small bowl, mix together the yogurt, cucumber, lemon juice, salt, and pepper.

TO MAKE THE CHEESEBURGER FILLING

2. In a pan, heat the oil over medium heat. Add the ground meat, salt, pepper, and garlic powder and cook, using a wooden spoon to break up the meat, for 5 to 7 minutes, until cooked through and no longer pink.

3. Add the cheddar, stir until combined, and continue to cook for 1 minute. Remove from the heat.

4. Divide the cheeseburger mixture between the pitas. Top with the tzatziki sauce and any optional toppings (if using) and serve.

5. For leftovers, store the filling and tzatziki sauce separately in a covered container for up to 3 days in the refrigerator. When ready to eat, reheat the filling in a pan until warm and add to the pita. The pita will get soggy if stored assembled.

COOKING TIP: To warm the pita breads, heat the pan over medium heat. Brush the pitas with olive oil on both sides and place in the pan. Heat for a couple of minutes on each side until warm.

Black Bean Burgers

MAKES 4 BURGERS

PREP TIME: 10 minutes

COOK TIME: 10 minutes

TOTAL TIME: 20 minutes

1 (15-ounce) can black beans, drained and rinsed

½ onion, finely diced

3 garlic cloves, minced

1 teaspoon ground cumin

1 tablespoon chili powder

1 teaspoon garlic powder

1 teaspoon salt

1 teaspoon ground black pepper

1 large egg, beaten

½ cup bread crumbs

¼ cup chopped fresh cilantro (optional)

2 tablespoons olive oil

4 hamburger buns or lettuce leaves

Optional toppings: avocado or salsa

These meatless burgers are oh-so-tasty with plenty of protein and fiber from the black beans. If you made extra spice blend for the Taco Tuesday recipe (see Tip, page 61), then you can save time here by using about 2 tablespoons of it in place of the cumin, chili powder, garlic powder, salt, and pepper.

1. Put the drained black beans in a bowl and blot them dry with a paper towel. Mash with a fork.

2. Add the onion, garlic, cumin, chili powder, garlic powder, salt, pepper, egg, bread crumbs, and cilantro (if using) and mix together. Using your hands, form the mixture into four patties.

3. In a pan, heat the oil over medium heat. Add the patties and cook for 5 minutes on each side.

4. Transfer to the hamburger buns or romaine leaves. Add toppings (if using) and serve.

MAKE IT FASTER: Make the black bean mixture ahead but do not form into patties. Place the mixture in a covered container and store in the fridge for up to 3 days. When ready to serve, form the mixture into patties and cook and serve as directed.

Brie and Berry Grilled Cheese

20-MINUTE MEAL · ONE AND DONE · VEGETARIAN

SERVES 1

PREP TIME: 5 minutes

COOK TIME: 15 minutes

TOTAL TIME: 20 minutes

1 cup blueberries, raspberries, or blackberries

¼ cup sugar

1 tablespoon freshly squeezed lemon juice

Pinch salt

2 slices bread

5 ounces Brie cheese, thinly sliced

2 tablespoons unsalted butter, at room temperature, divided

REMIX TIP: If you have any leftover onions from the Caramelized Onion–Stuffed Burgers (page 50), add them for an unexpected savory twist.

We're upgrading the classic grilled cheese with Brie and homemade jam. Making jam is very simple, and it can be stored in the fridge for up to 2 weeks. Use it on pancakes, oatmeal, or yogurt, or use it in the Vanilla Pudding with Berry Jam (page 124).

1. In a pan, combine the berries, sugar, lemon juice, and salt over low heat. Cook, stirring often, for 10 minutes. Using the back of a wooden spoon, mash the berries to help break down the fruit. Transfer the mixture to a container or jar with a lid.

2. Spread some jam on 1 slice of bread, layer with the Brie slices, and top with the second slice of bread.

3. Wipe the pan clean and heat 1 tablespoon of butter over medium heat. Add the sandwich and cook until the bottom is golden, about 2 minutes.

4. Spread the remaining 1 tablespoon of butter on the top of the bread. Using a spatula, carefully flip over the sandwich and cook until the bottom is golden and the Brie has melted, about 2 minutes. Cut in half and eat immediately.

Greek Pita Wraps with Tzatziki Sauce

HEALTHY · ONE AND DONE

SERVES 2

PREP TIME: 25 minutes

COOK TIME: 10 minutes

TOTAL TIME: 35 minutes

FOR THE CHICKEN

2 small boneless, skinless chicken breasts, cut into cubes or slices

¼ cup plain Greek yogurt

2 tablespoons freshly squeezed lemon juice

1 teaspoon salt

½ teaspoon ground black pepper

FOR THE TZATZIKI SAUCE

½ cup plain Greek yogurt

1 mini Persian cucumber, finely diced

1 tablespoon freshly squeezed lemon juice

Pinch salt

Pinch ground black pepper

Yogurt-marinated chicken provides fresh and bright flavors to stuff into a pita. The yogurt makes the chicken tender and juicy, and it will become one of your favorite ways to cook chicken. If you don't have pita on hand, make a lettuce wrap, or serve the chicken with a side dish instead.

FOR ASSEMBLY

1 tablespoon olive oil

2 pitas

Optional toppings: feta cheese, chopped lettuce, chopped fresh cilantro, and sliced tomato

TO MARINATE THE CHICKEN

1. In a bowl, mix together the chicken, yogurt, lemon juice, salt, and pepper. Set aside to marinate for 20 minutes.

TO MAKE THE TZATZIKI SAUCE

2. Meanwhile, in a small bowl, stir together the yogurt, cucumber, lemon juice, salt, and pepper. Set aside until serving.

TO ASSEMBLE THE PITAS

3. In a pan, heat the oil over medium-high heat. Add the chicken mixture and sauté for 8 to 10 minutes, until the chicken is fully cooked.

4. Spoon the chicken into the pitas. Top with the tzatziki sauce and any toppings (if using) and serve immediately.

SMART SHOPPING: Buy a larger pack of chicken breasts to save money. Use two chicken breasts for this recipe and store the remaining chicken in a zip-top plastic bag in the fridge for up to 2 days (or by the "use by" date) or freeze for up to 3 months. For recipes requiring cubed or sliced chicken, precut the chicken and portion it into separate zip-top plastic bags, and they'll be ready to cook.

Fried Egg and Bacon Sandwich

SERVES 1

PREP TIME: 5 minutes

COOK TIME: 15 minutes

TOTAL TIME: 20 minutes

½ tablespoon
  unsalted butter

2 slices bread

2 slices bacon

1 large egg

Pinch salt

Pinch ground black pepper

1 slice cheese or
  ½ cup shredded cheese
  of choice

1 tablespoon mayonnaise

2 slices tomato

¼ cup packed fresh
  spinach leaves

This breakfast staple is similar to a grilled cheese, but with an oozy egg instead of the cheese. Crispy bacon, fresh spinach, and tomato are added, making it a spin on another classic sandwich—the BLT.

1. In a pan, melt the butter over medium heat. Add the bread and toast both sides. Set aside.

2. Line a plate with paper towels. Add the bacon to the pan and cook until crisp to your liking. Transfer to the paper towels and set aside.

3. Carefully drain the fat from the pan, leaving about 1 tablespoon. Crack the egg into the pan and sprinkle with the salt and pepper. Cook until the egg white is set. Flip the egg and place the cheese on top. Cook the yolk to your desired firmness.

4. Spread the mayonnaise on the toast. Layer the egg, bacon, tomato, and spinach on one of the slices of toast and top with the second slice. Cut in half and eat immediately.

COOKING TIP: Don't pour bacon fat (or any oil) down the sink drain as it will clog the pipe. Instead, fold a piece of aluminum foil into the shape of a bowl and place it in the sink. Carefully pour the grease into the foil and let cool. Then you can wrap it up and throw it away.

Southwestern Chicken Lettuce Wraps

20-MINUTE MEAL · HEALTHY · ONE AND DONE

SERVES 2

PREP TIME: 10 minutes

COOK TIME: 10 minutes

TOTAL TIME: 20 minutes

2 small boneless, skinless chicken breasts, cut into cubes or strips

1 teaspoon salt

½ teaspoon ground black pepper

½ teaspoon garlic powder

½ teaspoon ground cumin

½ teaspoon chili powder

1 tablespoon olive oil

½ onion, thinly sliced

2 garlic cloves, minced

¼ cup sour cream or yogurt

Juice of 1 lime

6 romaine or iceberg lettuce leaves

Optional toppings: diced avocado, salsa, and sliced tomato

You can switch up these boldly flavored wraps by using any meat or skip the meat altogether to make this vegetarian. If you made extra of the spice mix from Taco Tuesday (see Tip, page 61), use 1 tablespoon of that instead of all the spices here for even speedier prep.

1. In a bowl, mix together the chicken, salt, pepper, garlic powder, cumin, and chili powder until the chicken is evenly coated.

2. In a pan, heat the oil over medium heat. Add the chicken and sauté for 5 minutes. Add the onion and garlic and sauté for another 3 minutes.

3. In a small bowl, whisk together the sour cream and lime juice.

4. To serve, divide the chicken mixture among the lettuce leaves. Top with the sour cream sauce and any toppings (if using) and serve.

REMIX TIP: For a spicier sauce, finely chop 1 chipotle pepper in adobo sauce or ½ jalapeño pepper and add it to the sour cream and lime juice.

Thai-Inspired Lettuce Wraps

HEALTHY · ONE AND DONE

SERVES 2

PREP TIME: 15 minutes

COOK TIME: 10 minutes

TOTAL TIME: 25 minutes

1 tablespoon olive oil

½ pound ground chicken, turkey, pork, or beef

2 garlic cloves, minced

1 teaspoon minced fresh ginger

1 carrot, diced or grated

1 red bell pepper, thinly sliced

2 tablespoons hoisin sauce

1 tablespoon peanut butter or any nut butter

1 scallion, thinly sliced

2 tablespoons chopped fresh cilantro

Juice of 1 lime

Romaine or iceberg lettuce leaves

Fresh and tangy flavors paired with crunchy vegetables make for a satisfying bite in these refreshing lettuce wraps. Use your favorite ground meat, such as chicken or turkey, or omit it altogether and double up on the vegetables. You can also make this into a bowl and serve it over chopped fresh lettuce or cooked rice.

1. In a pan, heat the oil over medium heat. Add the meat and cook, using a wooden spoon to break it up, for about 3 minutes, or until no longer pink.

2. Add the garlic, ginger, carrot, bell pepper, hoisin sauce, and peanut butter and cook, stirring often, for 3 minutes.

3. Turn off the heat and stir in the scallion, cilantro, and lime juice.

4. To serve, separate the lettuce leaves and place on a plate. Add a couple of spoonfuls of the filling into the center of each leaf and eat taco-style.

REMIX TIP: For a Korean-inspired flavor, omit the hoisin sauce and peanut butter and instead add 2 tablespoons of soy sauce, 1 teaspoon of sesame oil, and 1 teaspoon of brown sugar. For spice, add 1 tablespoon of gochujang (Korean red chili paste).

Taco Tuesday

20-MINUTE MEAL · ONE AND DONE

SERVES 2 TO 4
PREP TIME: 10 minutes
COOK TIME: 10 minutes
TOTAL TIME: 20 minutes

½ **pound ground beef or chicken**

½ **small onion, diced**

2 **garlic cloves, minced**

1 **tablespoon chili powder**

1 **teaspoon ground cumin**

½ **teaspoon garlic powder**

½ **teaspoon salt**

½ **teaspoon ground black pepper**

4 **flour or corn tortillas, for serving**

Optional toppings: shredded lettuce, chopped tomatoes, salsa, diced avocado, sour cream, and shredded cheese

Taco Tuesday is everyone's favorite night. Tacos are pretty simple to make, especially using just one pan, and you can get creative with the toppings. Of course, you don't need to eat them only on Tuesday; every day is a good day for tacos.

1. In a pan, cook the ground meat over medium-high heat, using a wooden spoon to break it up, for about 3 minutes, or until browned and no longer pink. Drain the grease from the pan, if needed.

2. Add the onion, garlic, chili powder, cumin, garlic powder, salt, and pepper and cook, stirring often, for 3 minutes. Remove from the heat, taste, and add more seasoning, if desired.

3. Fill the tortillas with the filling, add toppings (if using), and serve immediately.

MAKE IT FASTER: Save time by making the seasoning mix ahead of time. And while you're at it, make a double or triple amount of it and store in a small container, jar, or zip-top plastic bag. Use this mix to spice up meats and vegetables, or use it for seasoning the Black Bean Burgers (page 54) or the Southwestern Chicken Lettuce Wraps (page 59).

Leftovers Burritos

MAKES 2 BURRITOS

PREP TIME: 5 minutes

COOK TIME: 10 minutes

TOTAL TIME: 15 minutes

½ pound ground beef or chicken

½ onion, thinly sliced

1 (15-ounce) can black beans, drained and rinsed

1 (10-ounce) can red or green enchilada sauce

½ cup shredded cheese of choice

2 burrito-size flour tortillas

Optional toppings: chopped tomatoes, chopped fresh cilantro, diced avocado, and shredded lettuce

Make this burrito at the end of the week to use up leftovers. You can substitute chicken breasts for the ground beef, add cooked rice, or make it vegetarian by sautéing a variety of chopped vegetables along with the onions. Get creative!

1. Heat a pan over medium-high heat. Add the ground meat and cook, using a wooden spoon to break it up, for about 3 minutes, or until no longer pink. Drain off any excess fat, if needed.

2. Add the onion and sauté for 3 minutes.

3. Add the black beans and enchilada sauce and cook, stirring often, for 3 minutes.

4. Divide the filling between the tortillas, spooning it into the center. Top with cheese and any of the other toppings (if using). Fold in the sides, roll them up, and serve.

COOKING TIP: Eat one burrito now and wrap the extra in foil and store it in the fridge for up to 2 days. To reheat: In a pan, heat 1 tablespoon of oil over medium heat. Unwrap the foil and place the burrito in the pan, seam-side down. Cook for 3 to 4 minutes on both sides, until the tortilla is browned and the filling is warm.

Chicken and Veggie Quesadilla

SERVES 1

PREP TIME: 5 minutes

COOK TIME: 10 minutes

TOTAL TIME: 15 minutes

2 tablespoons olive oil, divided

½ onion, thinly sliced

1 bell pepper (any color), thinly sliced

1 cup shredded cooked chicken

1 cup shredded cheese of choice

1 tomato, chopped

Pinch salt

Pinch ground black pepper

¼ cup sour cream or plain Greek yogurt

2 large flour tortillas

Salsa, for serving

For those busy nights when you're short on time but need something filling, you can easily throw together this quesadilla filled with leftover store-bought rotisserie chicken from the Rotisserie Enchiladas (page 91). Customize this recipe by adding whatever vegetables you have on hand, or keep it simple with chicken and cheese.

1. In a pan, heat 1 tablespoon of oil over medium heat. Add the onion and bell pepper and sauté for about 3 minutes, or until the vegetables are soft. Turn off the heat.

2. Transfer the onion and bell pepper to a bowl. Add the chicken, cheese, tomato, salt, pepper, and sour cream and stir until combined.

3. In the pan, heat the remaining 1 tablespoon of oil over medium heat. Place 1 tortilla in the pan and spread the filling on top. Top with the remaining tortilla. Press down with a spatula and cook until the cheese is melted, and the tortilla is crisp, about 2 minutes on each side.

4. Cut into wedges and serve with salsa on the side.

REMIX TIP: Add chopped jalapeño peppers to the filling for some kick.

Deviled Egg Bites

5 OR FEWER INGREDIENTS · CHEAP EATS · HEALTHY · VEGETARIAN

MAKES 4 BITES

PREP TIME: 5 minutes

COOK TIME: 20 minutes

TOTAL TIME: 25 minutes

4 large eggs

2 tablespoons mayonnaise

1 teaspoon mustard

Pinch salt

Pinch ground black pepper

1 lettuce leaf, cut into 4 pieces

1 Roma (plum) tomato, cut into 4 slices, or 4 cherry tomatoes, halved

If you love deviled eggs, you'll love these egg bites, which are like delicious little sandwiches. Mixing the yolks with the mayonnaise and mustard results in a creamy texture in each bite. If you're not a mustard fan, feel free to omit it—they will still taste great. For spice, add a teaspoon of sriracha or a pinch of cayenne pepper to the filling.

1. Place the eggs in a pan and add enough water to cover halfway. Cover with a lid or aluminum foil and bring to a boil over high heat. Turn off the heat and leave the pan covered for 15 minutes. (Do not open the lid during this time.)

2. Carefully transfer the pan to the sink or remove the eggs with a slotted spoon or tongs and place them in a bowl. Rinse under cold running water until the eggs are cool.

3. Gently tap the shells on a hard surface and peel the shells. Cut the eggs in half lengthwise.

4. Remove the yolks and transfer into a small bowl. Set aside the whites. Add the mayonnaise, mustard, salt, and pepper to the bowl and mix together using a fork until combined.

5. Fill each egg white with the yolk mixture. Top four egg halves with the lettuce and tomato and sandwich the remaining egg halves on top. Eat immediately.

REMIX TIP: For extra protein, add chopped deli meat, or cook and crumble some bacon before cooking the eggs. Try adding other toppings such as sliced cheese, chopped cucumbers, or chopped pickles.

PORTOBELLO
MUSHROOM
STEAKS,
page 78

CHAPTER 5

Meatless Mains

Quinoa, Corn, Tomato, and Cucumber Salad

HEALTHY · ONE AND DONE · VEGAN

SERVES 2 TO 4

PREP TIME: 10 minutes

COOK TIME: 20 minutes

TOTAL TIME: 30 minutes

2 cups vegetable broth

1 cup quinoa

¼ cup olive oil

Juice of 1 lemon

2 tablespoons balsamic or red wine vinegar

2 garlic cloves, minced

Pinch salt, plus more to taste

Pinch ground black pepper, plus more to taste

1 (15-ounce) can corn, drained

2 cups packed fresh spinach or stemmed kale

1 tomato, diced, or 1 cup grape tomatoes, halved

1 cucumber, peeled and diced

¼ cup chopped fresh cilantro or parsley

This salad has a perfectly balanced combination of healthy, good-for-you ingredients. For a heartier option with more protein, add black beans or chickpeas. Make this refreshing salad for quick and nutritious lunches during the week.

1. In a pan, bring the broth to a boil over medium heat. Stir in the quinoa, cover with a lid or piece of aluminum foil, reduce the heat to low, and simmer for 20 minutes. Turn off the heat, remove the lid, and fluff the quinoa with a fork.

2. In a small bowl, whisk together the olive oil, lemon juice, vinegar, garlic, salt, and pepper.

3. In a separate bowl, combine the cooked quinoa, corn, spinach, tomato, cucumber, and cilantro. Pour the dressing over the top and toss to combine. Season with salt and pepper to taste.

4. Spoon into bowls and serve.

MAKE IT FASTER: The salad can be made ahead, stored in airtight containers, and refrigerated for up to 3 days.

Taco Salad

SERVES 2 OR 3

PREP TIME: 10 minutes

COOK TIME: 10 minutes

TOTAL TIME: 20 minutes

3 tablespoons olive oil

2 corn tortillas, cut into strips

Salt

1 (15-ounce) can black beans, drained and rinsed

1 (15-ounce) can corn, drained

3 cups chopped romaine lettuce

1 orange or yellow bell pepper, thinly sliced

2 tomatoes, diced

½ cup sour cream

½ cup salsa

You won't miss the meat in this taco salad because it's loaded with fresh veggies and topped with homemade tortilla strips.

1. Line a plate with paper towels.

2. In a pan, heat the oil over medium-high heat. When the oil is hot, carefully place the tortilla strips in the oil and fry until crispy.

3. Transfer the tortilla strips to the paper towels to drain. Sprinkle with salt.

4. Drain off the oil in the pan, leaving about 1 teaspoon. Reduce the heat to medium, add the beans and corn, and cook, stirring often, for 2 minutes.

5. Put the lettuce in a bowl or on a plate. Spoon the black bean and corn mixture on the lettuce and top with the bell pepper and tomatoes.

6. In a small bowl, mix together the sour cream and salsa. Pour over the salad, toss to combine, and top with the tortilla strips. Serve warm.

MAKE IT FASTER: Prepare everything ahead and store the vegetables, lettuce, and dressing in separate containers in the fridge for up to 3 days. Store the tortilla chips in an airtight container at room temperature. Assemble when ready to eat.

Sweet Potato Curry

HEALTHY · ONE AND DONE · VEGAN

SERVES 2

PREP TIME: 10 minutes

COOK TIME: 20 minutes

TOTAL TIME: 30 minutes

1 tablespoon olive oil

½ onion, diced

3 garlic cloves, minced

1 sweet potato, peeled and diced into ½-inch cubes

1 teaspoon curry powder

1 teaspoon ground cumin

1 teaspoon salt

½ teaspoon ground black pepper

1 (14.5-ounce) can diced tomatoes, undrained

1 (15-ounce) can chickpeas, drained and rinsed

½ cup coconut milk

2 cups cooked rice, warmed if made ahead, for serving

Chopped fresh cilantro, for garnish (optional)

This comforting meal has just the right balance of spicy and sweet with the curry powder, sweet potatoes, and coconut milk. If you don't have cooked rice available, cook it in the pan first and set aside. Double the rice you make for this dish, and save the other half to make the Veggie Fried Rice (page 77) on another day.

1. In a pan, heat the oil over medium heat. Add the onion and garlic and sauté for 2 minutes.

2. Add the sweet potato, curry powder, cumin, salt, and pepper and continue to sauté for 2 minutes. Stir in the tomatoes and their juices, the chickpeas, and coconut milk. Bring to a boil. Reduce the heat to low, cover, and simmer for about 15 minutes, or until the sweet potatoes are soft and tender.

3. Spoon the rice into bowls and top with the sweet potato mixture. If desired, garnish with cilantro. Serve warm.

COOKING TIP: Leftovers can be stored in an airtight container in the fridge for up to 4 days. If the curry seems dry when reheating, add 2 to 3 tablespoons of coconut milk or water and cook over medium heat until warm.

One-Pan Tomato Pasta

SERVES 2 TO 4

PREP TIME: 5 minutes

COOK TIME: 15 minutes

TOTAL TIME: 20 minutes

8 ounces spaghetti

½ onion, diced

2 garlic cloves, minced

1 tomato, diced, or 1 (14.5-ounce) can diced tomatoes

2½ cups vegetable broth or water

1 tablespoon olive oil

1 teaspoon salt, plus more to taste

½ teaspoon ground black pepper, plus more to taste

¼ cup chopped fresh basil

¼ cup grated Parmesan cheese (optional)

This is the easiest pasta recipe to make as the spaghetti is cooked in the pan along with the other ingredients. Once you've mastered the basic recipe, you can add different ingredients such as sliced smoked sausage or a handful of fresh spinach leaves. If you have leftovers at the end, use them in the Pasta Frittata (page 28).

1. In a pan, combine the spaghetti (break it up if needed to fit), onion, garlic, tomato, broth, oil, salt, and pepper. Bring to a boil over medium heat. Reduce the heat to low and simmer, stirring often to prevent the pasta from sticking, for 8 to 10 minutes, until the pasta is cooked.

2. Turn off the heat and stir in the basil and Parmesan (if using). Season with salt and pepper to taste.

3. Spoon into bowls and serve.

COOKING TIP: If the pasta is not cooked but the liquid has evaporated, add ¼ cup of water and continue to cook until the pasta is done.

Lemon-Garlic Pasta

20-MINUTE MEAL · CHEAP EATS · HEALTHY · ONE AND DONE · VEGETARIAN

SERVES 2 TO 4

PREP TIME: 5 minutes

COOK TIME: 15 minutes

TOTAL TIME: 20 minutes

8 ounces of your favorite pasta

2 garlic cloves, minced

½ teaspoon red pepper flakes

2½ cups vegetable broth or water

1 tablespoon olive oil

Juice of 1 lemon

1 teaspoon salt, plus more to taste

½ teaspoon ground black pepper, plus more to taste

¼ cup grated Parmesan cheese, plus more to taste

Chopped fresh basil or parsley leaves, for garnish (optional)

Another easy one-pan pasta dish that is tangy, simple, and light. You can also make different variations of the recipe by adding vegetables such as broccoli, peas, or asparagus with the pasta. Adjust the red pepper flakes to your preference. This dish is great as an entrée or as a side.

1. In a pan, combine the pasta, garlic, pepper flakes, broth, oil, lemon juice, salt, and black pepper. Bring to a boil over medium heat. Reduce the heat to low and simmer, stirring often to prevent the pasta from sticking, for 8 to 10 minutes, until the pasta is cooked. (The cooking time will vary depending on the type of pasta used; check the package instructions for more info.)

2. Turn off the heat and stir in the Parmesan. Taste and add more, if desired. Season with salt and pepper to taste and top with basil (if using).

3. Spoon into bowls and serve.

REMIX TIP: For a creamier sauce, stir in ¼ cup of heavy cream or coconut milk during the last minute of cooking.

Mediterranean Couscous

SERVES 2

PREP TIME: 15 minutes

COOK TIME: 5 minutes

TOTAL TIME: 20 minutes

FOR THE COUSCOUS

1 cup vegetable broth

1 teaspoon olive oil
or butter

½ teaspoon salt

1 cup couscous

FOR THE DRESSING

¼ cup olive oil

2 tablespoons red
wine vinegar or apple
cider vinegar

Juice of 1 lemon

2 garlic cloves, minced

½ teaspoon salt, plus more
to taste

½ teaspoon ground black
pepper, plus more to taste

Couscous is one of the quickest and easiest ingredients to cook. It's a tiny pasta made with semolina flour that steams in 5 minutes—and most varieties sold in stores are instant or quick-cooking. You can cook couscous in water, but when you cook it in broth it will have much greater depth of flavor.

FOR ASSEMBLY

½ small red onion, diced

1 tomato, diced

¼ cup kalamata olives,
pitted and sliced

1 Persian cucumber, peeled
and diced

¼ cup chopped fresh
parsley or cilantro

¼ cup crumbled feta
cheese (optional)

TO MAKE THE COUSCOUS

1. In a pan, combine the broth, oil, and salt and bring to a boil over medium heat.

2. Stir in the couscous, turn off the heat, and cover with a lid or piece of aluminum foil. Let steam for 4 to 5 minutes to allow the couscous to absorb the liquid.

CONTINUED >>

TO MAKE THE DRESSING

3. Meanwhile, in a separate small bowl, whisk together the oil, vinegar, lemon juice, garlic, salt, and pepper.

TO ASSEMBLE

4. Use a fork to fluff the couscous and to break up any clumps, then transfer to a bowl. Add the onion, tomato, olives, cucumber, and parsley and toss to combine.

5. Pour the dressing over the couscous and toss until combined. Taste and season with more salt and pepper, if desired. Top with feta cheese (if using) and serve.

COOKING TIP: If you purchased Israeli couscous (also called "pearl couscous"), which is bigger and takes longer to cook, follow the package directions for cooking time.

Ramen Stir-Fry

5 OR FEWER INGREDIENTS · 20-MINUTE MEAL · CHEAP EATS · ONE AND DONE · VEGAN

SERVES 1

PREP TIME: 10 minutes

COOK TIME: 10 minutes

TOTAL TIME: 20 minutes

2 cups plus 1 tablespoon water, divided

2 tablespoons hoisin sauce

1 teaspoon sesame oil

Pinch salt

Pinch ground black pepper

1 (3- to 4-ounce) package ramen noodles (any type, flavor packet discarded)

1 teaspoon olive oil

1 cup chopped vegetables, such as broccoli, cabbage, bell pepper, or carrots

The classic college meal gets a makeover with the addition of a homemade sauce and sautéed fresh vegetables. This recipe is great for using up any vegetables you have, but you can omit them altogether if you don't have any and don't feel like going out. Increase the serving size for a budget-friendly meal for a crowd.

1. In a small bowl, mix together 1 tablespoon of water, the hoisin sauce, sesame oil, salt, and pepper. Set aside.

2. In a pan, bring the remaining 2 cups of water to a boil over medium-high heat. Add the noodles and cook for 3 minutes. Drain and rinse with cold water and transfer to a bowl.

3. In the same pan, heat the olive oil over medium heat. Add the vegetables and stir-fry for about 3 minutes, or until soft.

4. Stir in the sauce and cook for 1 minute. Add the noodles and toss together until evenly coated.

5. Transfer to a bowl and serve.

SMART SHOPPING: Buy a bag of precut stir-fry vegetables or ready-to-use vegetables, such as shredded carrots or cabbage.

Cauliflower Mac and Cheese

5 OR FEWER INGREDIENTS · 20-MINUTE MEAL · HEALTHY · ONE AND DONE · VEGETARIAN

SERVES 1

PREP TIME: 10 minutes

COOK TIME: 10 minutes

TOTAL TIME: 15 minutes

3 cups water

2 cups cauliflower florets,
cut into small pieces

1 tablespoon
unsalted butter

½ teaspoon salt, plus more
to taste

½ teaspoon ground black
pepper, plus more to taste

½ teaspoon garlic powder,
plus more to taste

1 cup shredded cheddar
cheese, plus more to taste

2 tablespoons milk

When you have a mac and cheese craving, give this healthier cauliflower version a try. You'll still get the classic cheesy flavor but without the carbs. The traditional recipe uses cheddar cheese, but feel free to change it up and use Colby Jack, Monterey Jack, mozzarella, or a combination of several cheeses.

1. In a pan, bring the water to a boil over medium-high heat. Add the cauliflower, reduce the heat to medium, and cook for about 5 minutes, or until tender. Carefully drain the water from the pan.

2. Return the pan of cauliflower to low heat. Add the butter, salt, pepper, garlic powder, cheddar, and milk and stir until the cheese has melted. Taste and add more seasonings or cheese to your taste.

3. Spoon into a bowl and serve hot.

SUBSTITUTION: To make this dish using both cauliflower and elbow macaroni, boil 1 cup of macaroni in water for 2 minutes. Add 1 to 2 cups of cauliflower florets and boil together for 5 minutes, drain, and continue with the instructions from step 2, adding a bit more cheese and milk to the sauce, if needed.

Veggie Fried Rice

20-MINUTE MEAL · CHEAP EATS · HEALTHY · ONE AND DONE · VEGETARIAN

SERVES 1

PREP TIME: 5 minutes

COOK TIME: 10 minutes

TOTAL TIME: 15 minutes

1 tablespoon olive oil

1 small onion, diced

3 garlic cloves, minced

1 carrot, diced or grated

1 large egg

2 cups cooked white
  or brown rice,
  preferably cold

2 tablespoons soy sauce,
  plus more to taste

1 tablespoon sesame oil

½ teaspoon ground black
  pepper, plus more to taste

1 scallion, thinly sliced

Fried rice is a no-brainer to make when you have leftover cooked rice in the fridge. Freshly made rice will result in sticky clumps while stir-frying, so cold leftover rice will provide you with the best results. It's best to make the rice ahead of time and store it in an airtight container in the fridge until you're ready to cook (it should keep for up to 5 days).

1. In a pan, heat the olive oil over medium heat. Add the onion, garlic, and carrot and cook, stirring often, for 3 minutes.

2. Move the vegetables to the side of the pan and crack the egg in the empty half. Scramble using a circular motion, until cooked to your liking.

3. Break up any large clumps of rice and add to the pan. Add the soy sauce, sesame oil, pepper, and scallion and stir-fry for 2 minutes.

4. Taste and season with more pepper or soy sauce, if desired, and serve.

COOKING TIP: What if you don't have leftover rice already sitting in the fridge? Make the rice and spread it out on a large plate in an even layer and cool completely. Pop it in the freezer for 15 to 20 minutes or in the refrigerator for about 1 hour.

Portobello Mushroom Steaks

5 OR FEWER INGREDIENTS · 20-MINUTE MEAL · HEALTHY

SERVES 2

PREP TIME: 10 minutes
COOK TIME: 10 minutes
TOTAL TIME: 20 minutes

1 tablespoon olive oil

1½ teaspoons soy sauce, tamari, or coconut aminos

1½ teaspoons balsamic vinegar

¼ teaspoon ground black pepper

½ teaspoon garlic powder

2 portobello mushrooms, cleaned and stems discarded

You'll love these flavorful and meaty portobello mushroom steaks. Serve as a main dish with a vegetable or grain on the side, or serve it in a bun as a meatless burger. You can also chop it up after cooking and add it to bowls or wraps. Double the batch, store in an airtight container in the fridge, and add to meals all week.

1. In a large dish or bowl, mix together the olive oil, soy sauce, balsamic vinegar, pepper, and garlic powder. Place the mushrooms in the dish and brush the mixture over all sides of the mushrooms. Let sit for about 5 minutes to marinate.

2. Heat a pan over medium heat. Place the mushrooms in the pan and cook for 3 to 5 minutes on each side.

3. Transfer to a plate and serve immediately.

COOKING TIP: Don't wash the mushrooms under running water. Mushrooms absorb water like a sponge. The best method is to clean the surface with a damp paper towel.

Healthy Buddha Bowls

20-MINUTE MEAL · HEALTHY · ONE AND DONE · VEGAN

SERVES 2

PREP TIME: 10 minutes
COOK TIME: 10 minutes
TOTAL TIME: 20 minutes

¼ cup water

1 tablespoon soy sauce

1 tablespoon hoisin sauce

1 teaspoon light
brown sugar

1 teaspoon sesame oil

1 teaspoon cornstarch

Pinch ground black pepper

1 tablespoon olive oil

7 ounces (half a 14-ounce)
package firm or extra-firm
tofu, cubed

1 garlic clove, minced

1 cup chopped broccoli or
cauliflower

1 carrot, thinly sliced
or grated

1 cup chopped cabbage

A Buddha bowl is a one-bowl vegan meal that includes fresh vegetables, rice, legumes, or plant-based proteins. You can customize by adding any vegetables you have available. Save the other half of the tofu package for the Spicy Vegan Lettuce Wraps (page 43).

1. In a small bowl, mix together the water, soy sauce, hoisin sauce, brown sugar, sesame oil, cornstarch, and pepper. Set aside.

2. In a pan, heat the olive oil over medium-high heat. Add the tofu and stir-fry for 3 to 4 minutes, until lightly browned.

3. Add the garlic and stir-fry for 30 seconds. Add the broccoli, carrot, and cabbage and stir-fry for about 5 minutes, or until the vegetables are tender.

4. Stir in the sauce and stir-fry for 1 more minute.

5. Spoon into bowls and serve warm.

COOKING TIP: For crispier tofu, dry the tofu with paper towels to remove excess moisture before cutting into cubes. Add 1 tablespoon of cornstarch to a plate and toss the tofu cubes with the cornstarch before cooking.

Vegetarian Chili

SERVES 2 OR 3

PREP TIME: 10 minutes

COOK TIME: 25 minutes

TOTAL TIME: 35 minutes

1 tablespoon olive oil

1 onion, diced

1 bell pepper (any color), diced

2 garlic cloves, minced

1 tablespoon chili powder

1 tablespoon ground cumin

1 teaspoon paprika

1 teaspoon salt, plus more to taste

1 teaspoon ground black pepper, plus more to taste

1 (15-ounce) can kidney beans, drained and rinsed

1 (15-ounce) can pinto beans, drained and rinsed

1 (14.5-ounce) can diced tomatoes, undrained

The best vegetarian chili is one that is full of flavor and leaves you completely satisfied. Grab a big bowl, top with your favorite garnishes, and enjoy this perfect meal any night of the week. Feel free to swap in your favorite beans.

1. In a pan, heat the oil over medium heat. Add the onion and bell pepper and sauté for about 3 minutes, or until the vegetables are soft and the onion is translucent.

2. Add the garlic, chili powder, cumin, paprika, salt, and pepper and sauté for about 1 minute.

3. Stir in the kidney beans, pinto beans, and tomatoes and their juices. Bring to a boil over medium-high heat. Reduce the heat to low and simmer, stirring often, for 20 minutes.

4. Taste, adjust the seasonings, and serve.

REMIX TIP: For a heartier dish, add 1 small diced sweet potato with the beans. Another option is to add 1 cup of rice or quinoa, along with 1½ cups of water or broth when you add the beans.

CHICKEN
CACCIATORE,
page 93

Seafood and Poultry

Pan-Fried Cajun Shrimp

20-MINUTE MEAL · HEALTHY · ONE AND DONE

SERVES 2

PREP TIME: 5 minutes
COOK TIME: 10 minutes
TOTAL TIME: 15 minutes

1 tablespoon unsalted
   butter or olive oil

½ pound large shrimp,
   peeled and deveined

½ small onion, thinly sliced

1 red bell pepper,
   thinly sliced

1 teaspoon Cajun or Creole
   seasoning

2 garlic cloves, minced

Juice of ½ lemon

Chopped fresh parsley, for
   garnish (optional)

Add some kick to your shrimp in this Cajun-flavored dish that is low-carb and healthy. Enjoy it on its own, or in a bowl over cooked rice or quinoa, or as tacos, as a salad over some mixed greens, or wrapped in large lettuce leaves. Any way you serve these shrimp, they will be delicious!

1. In a pan, heat the butter over medium-high heat. Add the shrimp and sauté for about 3 minutes, or until the shrimp are pink. Transfer to a plate and set aside.

2. Add the onion, bell pepper, and Cajun seasoning to the pan and sauté for 3 minutes.

3. Return the shrimp to the pan, add the garlic and lemon juice and sauté for 1 more minute.

4. Transfer to plates, garnish with the parsley (if using), and serve.

SMART SHOPPING: What's the difference between Cajun and Creole seasoning? While all brands are different, Cajun generally includes more types of pepper, such as white, black, and red pepper, while Creole includes more herb varieties, such as oregano, rosemary, and thyme.

Shrimp Jambalaya

SERVES 2 OR 3

PREP TIME: 10 minutes

COOK TIME: 25 minutes

TOTAL TIME: 35 minutes

1 tablespoon olive oil

1 smoked or andouille
  sausage, cut into
  ¼-inch-thick rounds

½ onion, diced

1 celery stalk, diced

1 green bell pepper, diced

2 garlic cloves, minced

1 cup long-grain white rice

1 tablespoon Cajun or
  Creole seasoning

2 cups chicken broth

1 (14.5-ounce) can diced
  tomatoes, undrained

½ pound medium to large
  shrimp, peeled and
  deveined

Salt

Ground black pepper

Jambalaya is a Southern one-pot dish typically made with sausage and either chicken or shrimp (or both) and simmered with rice, vegetables, and seasonings. It is hearty and flavorful and ideal for sharing.

1. In a pan, heat the oil over medium-high heat. Add the sausage and sauté for 2 minutes, or until browned.

2. Add the onion, celery, bell pepper, and garlic and sauté for 3 minutes.

3. Stir in the rice, Cajun seasoning, broth, and tomatoes with their juices and bring to a boil. Reduce the heat to low, cover with a lid or aluminum foil, and simmer for 17 to 20 minutes, until the rice is cooked through.

4. Stir in the shrimp and continue to cook for 3 minutes. Turn off the heat and season with salt and pepper to taste. Serve hot.

REMIX TIP: Omit the shrimp, add cubed boneless, skinless chicken breasts, and sauté with the sausage. For more spice, add 1 chopped jalapeño pepper along with the onion.

Garlic-Soy Shrimp and Veggie Stir-Fry

HEALTHY · ONE AND DONE

SERVES 2

PREP TIME: 20 minutes

COOK TIME: 10 minutes

TOTAL TIME: 30 minutes

½ pound medium to large shrimp, peeled and deveined

2 tablespoons soy sauce

1 tablespoon water

1 teaspoon sesame oil

1 teaspoon light brown sugar

2 garlic cloves, minced

1 tablespoon olive oil

1 carrot, thinly sliced or grated

1 cup chopped broccoli florets

1 red bell pepper, thinly sliced

1 scallion, thinly sliced, for garnish (optional)

Shrimp marinated in garlic and soy sauce gets stir-fried with colorful veggies for a quick and satisfying meal. Swap in other vegetables—such as sliced mushrooms, green beans, or snap peas—and other protein, such as diced chicken or cubed tofu.

1. In a medium bowl, toss together the shrimp, soy sauce, water, sesame oil, brown sugar, and garlic until evenly coated. Set aside to marinate for 10 minutes.

2. In a pan, heat the olive oil over medium heat. Add the shrimp and stir-fry for 2 minutes. Transfer to a plate and set aside. The shrimp will not be cooked through.

3. Add the carrot, broccoli, and bell pepper to the pan and stir-fry for 2 to 3 minutes, until the vegetables are tender. Return the shrimp to the pan and sauté for 1 to 2 minutes, until the shrimp is cooked.

4. Transfer to plates, garnish with the scallion (if using), and serve.

REMIX TIP: Omit the marinade and the marinating step. Then when you cook the shrimp the first time, add the juice of 1 lemon, 2 minced garlic cloves, and 1 tablespoon of water. Continue with the recipe as written.

Pan-Seared Salmon with Spinach and Tomatoes

5 OR FEWER INGREDIENTS · 20-MINUTE MEAL · HEALTHY · ONE AND DONE

SERVES 2

PREP TIME: 5 minutes

COOK TIME: 15 minutes

TOTAL TIME: 20 minutes

2 tablespoons olive oil

2 salmon fillets (6 ounces each)

Pinch salt

Pinch ground black pepper

2 garlic cloves, minced

1 cup grape tomatoes or 1 tomato, diced

2 cups packed baby spinach

½ lemon, cut into slices

Pan-frying salmon brings out its delicious flavor and appealing texture and keeps it tender and moist. For a crisp skin, make sure you pat the salmon dry with a paper towel before cooking and wait until it easily releases from the pan before flipping it over.

1. In a pan, heat the oil over medium-high heat. Season the salmon with salt and pepper and place skin-side down in the pan. Cook for about 3 minutes, or until it releases easily from the pan. Flip the salmon over and cook for 2 more minutes. Transfer the salmon to a plate and set aside.

2. Add the garlic and tomatoes to the pan and cook for 1 minute. Stir in the spinach.

3. Return the salmon to the pan, top with lemon slices, reduce the heat to low, and simmer for about 1 more minute, or until the salmon is fully cooked.

4. Transfer to plates and serve.

SMART SHOPPING: Wild salmon in the United States is typically harvested in the Pacific Ocean and only available fresh in the summer months. During the other months, it's sold as frozen or previously frozen. Wild is usually more expensive than farmed salmon, but both are delicious, so buy whatever fits your budget.

Creamy Parmesan Chicken

SERVES 2
PREP TIME: 5 minutes
COOK TIME: 15 minutes
TOTAL TIME: 20 minutes

4 boneless, skinless chicken thighs

1 teaspoon salt

1 teaspoon ground black pepper

1 tablespoon olive oil

2 garlic cloves, minced

1 tomato, diced

¼ cup heavy cream

¼ cup grated Parmesan cheese

1 cup packed spinach leaves

The chicken in this low-carb dish is pan-fried to perfection and simmered in a creamy garlic and Parmesan cheese sauce. Chicken thighs are used here, but feel free to use breasts, especially if they are on sale. This dish can be served on its own, with some cooked pasta, or over a bed of lettuce or mixed greens.

1. Pat the chicken thighs dry with paper towels. Sprinkle with the salt and pepper on both sides.

2. In a pan, heat the oil over medium-high heat. Add the chicken and cook until browned and cooked through, 4 to 5 minutes per side. Transfer the chicken to a plate and set aside.

3. Reduce the heat to low, add the garlic, and sauté for 30 seconds. Add the tomato, cream, and Parmesan and cook, stirring constantly, for 1 minute. Return the chicken to the pan, add the spinach, and cook for about 2 minutes to wilt the spinach.

4. Transfer to plates and serve hot.

MAKE IT FASTER: This recipe can be made ahead as directed, but omit the Parmesan. Store in an airtight container in the fridge for up to 3 days. When you are ready to eat, transfer everything to a pan, add the Parmesan, and simmer over medium heat, stirring often, until heated through.

Lemon-Garlic Chicken

20-MINUTE MEAL · HEALTHY · ONE AND DONE

SERVES 2

PREP TIME: 5 minutes

COOK TIME: 15 minutes

TOTAL TIME: 20 minutes

4 boneless, skinless chicken thighs

Pinch salt

Pinch ground black pepper

1 tablespoon olive oil

1 tablespoon unsalted butter

2 garlic cloves, minced

½ cup chicken broth

Juice of ½ lemon

Chopped fresh parsley, for garnish (optional)

This tender and juicy chicken would pair well with a side of Mediterranean Couscous (page 73) or Quinoa, Corn, Tomato, and Cucumber Salad (page 68). The chicken broth keeps the chicken moist, especially when reheating. For a creamier option, add ¼ cup of plain yogurt or coconut milk along with the broth.

1. Pat the chicken thighs dry with paper towels and sprinkle with the salt and pepper on both sides.

2. In a pan, heat the oil over medium-high heat. Add the chicken and cook for 4 minutes on each side. Transfer to a plate and set aside.

3. Add the butter and garlic to the pan and sauté for 30 seconds. Add the chicken broth and lemon juice, return the chicken to the pan, and bring to a simmer. Continue to cook, turning the chicken over to coat with the sauce, about 2 minutes.

4. Transfer to plates, garnish with parsley (if using), and serve.

SMART SHOPPING: Buy a pack of eight chicken thighs, store half of them in an airtight container in the fridge to use in another recipe later in the week, or make a double batch of this recipe and store the leftovers in the fridge for up to 3 days.

Chicken and Broccoli Pasta

SERVES 2 TO 4

PREP TIME: 5 minutes

COOK TIME: 15 minutes

TOTAL TIME: 20 minutes

2 boneless, skinless chicken breasts, cubed

Pinch salt, plus more to taste

Pinch ground black pepper, plus more to taste

1 tablespoon olive oil or unsalted butter

8 ounces penne or rotini pasta

2 garlic cloves, minced

2 cups chicken broth or water

½ cup heavy cream, milk, or coconut milk

2 cups broccoli florets

¼ cup grated Parmesan cheese

This is a healthier take on classic fettuccine Alfredo, with less heavy cream and added broccoli. Using smaller pasta shapes instead of the long fettuccine saves on cooking time. Swap the broccoli for cauliflower or asparagus or omit altogether.

1. Pat the chicken breasts dry with paper towels. Sprinkle with the salt and pepper on both sides.

2. In a pan, heat the oil over medium-high heat. Add the chicken and sauté for about 4 minutes, until browned. Transfer to a plate and set aside.

3. Add the pasta, garlic, broth, and cream to the pan and stir to combine. Bring to a boil, then reduce the heat to low and simmer, stirring often, for 6 minutes.

4. Add the broccoli and chicken and continue to cook for about 2 more minutes, or until the pasta is cooked through.

5. Turn off the heat, stir in the Parmesan, and serve.

REMIX TIP: For traditional fettuccine Alfredo, omit the broccoli. Use fettuccine pasta, add 1 tablespoon of unsalted butter, 1 cup of heavy cream, and 1½ cups of broth. Cook for 10 to 12 minutes, until the pasta is cooked through.

Rotisserie Enchiladas

5 OR FEWER INGREDIENTS · 20-MINUTE MEAL · ONE AND DONE

SERVES 1

PREP TIME: 12 minutes

COOK TIME: 8 minutes

TOTAL TIME: 20 minutes

1½ cups shredded
   rotisserie chicken

1 (10-ounce) can red
   or green enchilada
   sauce, divided

1 cup shredded cheese of
   choice, divided

4 corn tortillas

Optional toppings:
   sour cream, chopped
   tomatoes, and chopped
   fresh cilantro

For quick meals all week, save any leftover rotisserie chicken for the Chicken and Veggie Quesadilla (page 63) or the Southwestern Chicken (page 92).

1. In a bowl, mix together the chicken, ¼ cup of enchilada sauce, and ½ cup of cheese.

2. In a pan over low heat, warm the tortillas on each side until pliable to make them easier to roll.

3. Place a tortilla flat on a plate. Add a spoonful of the chicken mixture to the center of the tortilla. Roll it up tightly and place it seam-side down in the pan. Repeat with the remaining tortillas and filling. Top with the remaining enchilada sauce and cheese.

4. Place a lid or aluminum foil over the pan and cook over medium heat for about 5 minutes, or until the sauce is bubbling.

5. Transfer to a plate, add toppings (if using), and serve.

SUBSTITUTION: To use boneless, skinless chicken breasts instead, cut into small pieces. Heat 1 tablespoon of olive oil in a pan over medium heat and sauté the chicken for a few minutes until cooked through. When cool enough to handle, toss with the enchilada sauce and cheese and assemble the enchiladas as directed.

Southwestern Chicken

5 OR FEWER INGREDIENTS · 20-MINUTE MEAL · HEALTHY · ONE AND DONE

SERVES 2

PREP TIME: 5 minutes

COOK TIME: 10 minutes

TOTAL TIME: 15 minutes

1½ **cups shredded cooked chicken**

1 **(15-ounce) can black beans, drained and rinsed**

1 **cup salsa**

1 **teaspoon chili powder**

½ **teaspoon salt**

½ **teaspoon ground black pepper**

Optional toppings: shredded cheese, sliced scallions, and chopped fresh cilantro

This recipe can be made with leftover cooked shredded chicken from the Rotisserie Enchiladas (page 91) to save time, or you can use ground chicken instead. To cook ground chicken, heat 1 tablespoon of olive oil over medium heat in a pan, add ½ pound of ground chicken, and cook until browned and cooked through.

1. In a pan, combine the shredded chicken, black beans, salsa, chili powder, salt, and pepper and mix together over medium-high heat.

2. Reduce the heat to low and simmer, stirring often, for 5 minutes.

3. Transfer to plates, add toppings (if using), and serve.

REMIX TIP: For a heartier meal, add rice: Add 2 cups of chicken broth along with the rest of the ingredients and bring to a boil. Add 1 cup of uncooked rice and simmer over low heat for 17 to 20 minutes, until the rice is cooked through.

Chicken Cacciatore

SERVES 2

PREP TIME: 10 minutes

COOK TIME: 20 minutes

TOTAL TIME: 30 minutes

4 boneless, skinless chicken thighs

Pinch salt, plus more to taste

Pinch ground black pepper, plus more to taste

¼ cup all-purpose or gluten-free flour

1 tablespoon olive oil

1 tablespoon unsalted butter

½ onion, diced

2 garlic cloves, minced

1 bell pepper (any color), sliced

½ cup chicken broth

1 (14.5-ounce) can diced or crushed tomatoes, undrained

1 tablespoon capers, drained

1 teaspoon dried oregano

Chicken cacciatore is traditionally served with crusty bread or polenta, but it can also be served on its own or with cooked pasta. Boneless chicken thighs are used here for a faster cooking time.

1. Pat the chicken thighs dry with paper towels. Season with the salt and pepper. Spread the flour on a plate and dredge the chicken on both sides. Shake off any excess flour.

2. In a pan, heat the oil and butter over medium-high heat. Add the chicken and cook for 4 to 5 minutes, until browned on both sides. Transfer to a plate and set aside.

3. Add the onion, garlic, and bell pepper and sauté for 3 minutes. Add the broth, tomatoes with their juices, capers, and oregano. Return the chicken to the pan, reduce the heat to medium-low, and simmer for 5 minutes, or until the chicken is cooked through. Serve hot.

SUBSTITUTION: Boneless, skinless chicken breasts can be used, but thighs will provide deeper flavor.

Teriyaki Chicken and Vegetable Stir-Fry

20-MINUTE MEAL · HEALTHY · ONE AND DONE

SERVES 1

PREP TIME: 10 minutes
COOK TIME: 10 minutes
TOTAL TIME: 20 minutes

1½ tablespoons olive oil, divided

1 boneless, skinless chicken breast, cubed

1 tablespoon soy sauce

1 tablespoon water

1 teaspoon sesame oil

1 tablespoon light brown sugar or honey

2 garlic cloves, minced

1 tablespoon cornstarch

2 cups chopped vegetables, such as broccoli, carrots, bell pepper, or mushrooms

Sesame seeds or thinly sliced scallions, for garnish (optional)

You'll love this homemade version of a favorite take-out dish. To save time, make the sauce while the chicken is cooking. This dish can be served on its own or with cooked rice, couscous, or quinoa.

1. In a pan, heat 1 tablespoon of oil over medium heat. Add the chicken and stir-fry for about 4 minutes, until browned. Turn off the heat, transfer the chicken to a plate, and set aside.

2. In a small bowl, whisk together the soy sauce, water, sesame oil, brown sugar, garlic, and cornstarch and whisk until well combined. Set aside.

3. If the pan is dry, add the remaining ½ tablespoon oil and heat over medium heat. Add the vegetables and stir-fry for about 2 minutes, or until tender.

4. Return the chicken to the pan, pour in the sauce, and stir-fry for 2 minutes to heat through.

5. If desired, garnish with sesame seeds or scallions. Serve hot.

SMART SHOPPING: In the produce section of most grocery stores, you can find washed, cut-up, ready-to-use stir-fry vegetables. This is a great option to save time and money and to have less food waste.

Healthy Orange Chicken

20-MINUTE MEAL · HEALTHY · ONE AND DONE

SERVES 2
PREP TIME: 5 minutes
COOK TIME: 15 minutes
TOTAL TIME: 20 minutes

2 boneless, skinless chicken breasts, cut into cubes

Pinch salt

Pinch ground black pepper

¼ cup cornstarch

1 tablespoon olive oil

2 garlic cloves, minced

¼ cup orange juice, preferably freshly squeezed

2 tablespoons soy sauce

2 tablespoons honey

Sliced scallions, for garnish (optional)

This homemade version of a popular take-out favorite is lightened up without losing any of the flavors. The chicken is coated with cornstarch, sautéed, and simmered in an orange-soy sauce, which makes it healthier than the fried version typically served at restaurants. Try this over steamed rice or cauliflower rice.

1. Pat the chicken thighs dry with paper towels. Season with the salt and pepper. Spread the cornstarch on a plate and toss the chicken in the cornstarch until evenly coated. Shake off any excess cornstarch.

2. In a pan, heat the oil over medium heat. Add the chicken and stir-fry for 3 to 4 minutes. Add the garlic and stir-fry for 20 seconds.

3. Add the orange juice, soy sauce, and honey and stir until combined. Reduce the heat to low and simmer for 8 to 10 minutes, until the chicken is cooked through.

4. Transfer to plates and garnish with scallions (if using). Serve hot.

SUBSTITUTION: For a vegetarian option, pat firm or extra-firm tofu dry with paper towels and cut into small cubes. Toss them in the cornstarch and follow the recipe as written.

KOREAN-INSPIRED BEEF BOWL,
page 104

CHAPTER 7

Pork and Beef

· ·

Sausage and Peppers with Caramelized Onions

20-MINUTE MEAL · HEALTHY · ONE AND DONE

SERVES 2
PREP TIME: 5 minutes
COOK TIME: 15 minutes
TOTAL TIME: 20 minutes

2 tablespoons olive
  oil, divided

½ pound pork sausage,
  bulk or links (casings
  removed)

½ onion, sliced

½ teaspoon salt

½ teaspoon ground
  black pepper

1 tablespoon
  balsamic vinegar

1 bell pepper (any
  color), diced

1 tomato, diced

2 garlic cloves, minced

Caramelizing onions (sautéing until brown) brings out their natural sweetness, which adds a nice balance to this dish, especially when it's combined with the spice in the sausage.

1. In a pan, heat 1 tablespoon of olive oil over medium-high heat. Add the sausage and cook, breaking up the meat with a wooden spoon, until browned, about 3 minutes. Transfer to a plate and set aside.

2. Add the remaining 1 tablespoon of olive oil and the onion to the pan and sauté for 2 minutes. Add the salt, pepper, and balsamic vinegar and continue to sauté for about 5 minutes, or until the onions caramelize and become soft and browned.

3. Add the sausage, bell pepper, tomato, and garlic and sauté for about 2 minutes, or until the sausage is cooked through and the vegetables are tender. Serve warm.

SMART SHOPPING: The different colors of bell peppers have different flavor profiles. Red peppers are the sweetest and taste great eaten raw. Orange and yellow peppers are also on the sweet side. Green bell peppers have a sharp, bitter taste when eaten raw, but cooking mellows out their flavor.

Pork Chops with Apples

20-MINUTE MEAL · HEALTHY · ONE AND DONE

SERVES 2

PREP TIME: 5 minutes

COOK TIME: 15 minutes

TOTAL TIME: 20 minutes

2 bone-in pork chops or boneless pork loin chops

Salt

Ground black pepper

1 tablespoon unsalted butter

1 apple, cored and cut into ¼-inch-thick slices

½ onion, thinly sliced

2 garlic cloves, minced

¼ cup chicken broth or water

1 teaspoon balsamic vinegar

Pork chops and apples make a great fall flavor combination. Any apple will work, such as Honey Crisp, Fuji, Pink Lady, or Granny Smith. For added spice, season the pork chops with 1 tablespoon of chili powder.

1. Pat the pork chops dry with paper towels. Season with salt and pepper on both sides.

2. In a pan, heat the butter over medium-high heat. Add the pork chops and cook for about 3 minutes on each side, until browned. Transfer to a plate and set aside.

3. Add the apple, onion, and garlic to the pan and cook for 3 to 4 minutes, until the apple begins to soften.

4. Add a pinch of salt and pepper. Stir in the chicken broth and balsamic vinegar, using a wooden spoon to scrape up any browned bits from the bottom of the pan. Return the pork chops to the pan and continue to cook for about 4 minutes, or until cooked through.

5. Transfer to a plate and serve warm.

SMART SHOPPING: Choose pork chops that are between ½ and 1 inch thick. This will ensure that they cook evenly and within the cooking time provided.

Provençal Pork Chops

SERVES 2

PREP TIME: 5 minutes

COOK TIME: 15 minutes

TOTAL TIME: 20 minutes

1 tablespoon olive oil or butter

2 boneless pork loin chops, ½ to 1 inch thick

Salt

Ground black pepper

½ cup chicken broth

½ onion, thinly sliced or cut into wedges

2 small red or gold potatoes, cut into ¼-inch-thick slices

1 cup grape tomatoes, halved, or 1 tomato, diced

2 tablespoons pitted kalamata olives or capers (optional)

Chopped fresh parsley, for garnish (optional)

Welcome to the flavors of Provence in these pan-seared pork chops simmered with vegetables in chicken broth, which keeps them moist. Serve the chops on their own or over a bed of spinach leaves or couscous to absorb the yummy sauce. To cook couscous, check out Mediterranean Couscous (page 73).

1. In a pan, heat the oil over medium-high heat. Season the pork on both sides with salt and pepper. Add the pork chops to the pan and cook until browned, about 2 minutes per side.

2. Add the chicken broth, onion, potatoes, tomatoes, olives, and a pinch of salt and pepper.

3. Cover with a lid or aluminum foil, reduce the heat to low, and simmer for 7 to 8 minutes, until the pork is cooked and the potatoes are tender. Taste and add more salt and pepper, if desired.

4. Transfer to plates, garnish with the parsley (if using), and serve.

REMIX TIP: To make a creamy sauce, stir in 2 tablespoons of heavy cream, sour cream, or plain yogurt after the pork chops and vegetables are cooked.

Cauliflower Rice Pilaf

20-MINUTE MEAL · HEALTHY · ONE AND DONE

SERVES 2 OR 3

PREP TIME: 5 minutes

COOK TIME: 15 minutes

TOTAL TIME: 20 minutes

1 tablespoon olive oil

2 boneless pork loin chops, cubed

5 ounces fresh pork or beef Mexican chorizo, casings removed

½ onion, diced

1 cup cauliflower rice

1 bell pepper (any color), diced

2 garlic cloves, minced

1 tomato, diced

¼ cup chicken broth or water

1 teaspoon paprika

Pinch salt

Pinch ground black pepper

This low-carb dish is inspired by paella, a classic Spanish dish made of rice, but uses cauliflower rice instead. It's versatile, so feel free to use chicken or seafood or use a plant-based sausage for a vegetarian option.

1. In a pan, heat the oil over medium heat. Add the pork and chorizo and sauté for 1 minute.

2. Add the onion, cauliflower rice, bell pepper, and garlic and sauté for 2 minutes.

3. Add the tomato, chicken broth, paprika, salt, and pepper and stir until combined. Cover with a lid or aluminum foil, reduce the heat to low, and simmer for 7 to 8 minutes, until the pork is cooked through.

4. Spoon onto plates and serve.

SMART SHOPPING: There are two types of chorizo. Fresh chorizo, usually sold as Mexican chorizo, is made with beef or pork and needs to be cooked first. It comes in a casing, but the casing is not always edible. You can also find plant-based chorizo made with soy. Spanish chorizo is a hard-cured and dried meat, like salami. It comes pre-cooked and can be eaten as is.

Meatballs in Marinara Sauce

HEALTHY · ONE AND DONE

SERVES 2

PREP TIME: 15 minutes

COOK TIME: 30 minutes

TOTAL TIME: 45 minutes

FOR THE MEATBALLS

½ **pound ground beef, pork, or turkey**

¼ **onion, grated or finely chopped**

2 garlic cloves, minced

¼ **cup bread crumbs**

2 tablespoons grated Parmesan cheese

1 large egg

2 tablespoons milk

2 tablespoons chopped fresh parsley

1 teaspoon garlic powder

1 teaspoon salt

1 teaspoon ground black pepper

½ **cup all-purpose flour**

2 tablespoons olive oil

Make these once, and they will become your favorite go-to meatball recipe. Meatballs are great for adding to soups, sub sandwiches, or pasta, but they're also hearty enough to have on their own. Serve with some crusty bread to slather up all of that yummy, homemade marinara sauce.

TO MAKE THE MEATBALLS

1. In a large bowl, mix together the ground meat, onion, garlic, bread crumbs, Parmesan, egg, milk, parsley, garlic powder, salt, and pepper and gently mix together just until combined.

2. Spread the flour on a plate or bowl. Form the meat mixture into 1-inch meatballs, wetting your hands with water to prevent sticking if needed, and roll the meatballs in the flour to coat. Shake off any excess flour.

3. In a pan, heat the oil over medium heat. Working in batches, cook the meatballs for about 5 minutes, or until browned on all sides. Transfer to a plate and set aside.

1 tablespoon olive oil
  (optional)

¼ onion, diced or grated

2 garlic cloves, minced

1 (14.5-ounce) can crushed
  tomatoes

Salt

Ground black pepper

TO MAKE THE MARINARA SAUCE

4. If the pan is dry, add the oil and heat over medium heat. Add the onion and garlic and sauté for 3 minutes, scraping the bottom of the pan with a wooden spoon to get any browned bits.

5. Stir in the tomatoes and bring to a boil. Reduce the heat to low, return the meatballs to the pan, cover, and simmer, stirring often, for 15 to 20 minutes, until the meatballs are cooked through. Taste the sauce and add salt and pepper, if desired.

6. To serve, divide the meatballs between bowls and top with the marinara.

REMIX TIP: For Asian-inspired meatballs, to the meat mixture add ½-inch grated or minced fresh ginger, 1 tablespoon of soy sauce, and 2 tablespoons of minced scallion. Omit the Parmesan and parsley. Form and cook as directed, then divide between bowls, but skip the marinara.

Korean-Inspired Beef Bowl

20-MINUTE MEAL · ONE AND DONE

SERVES 1

PREP TIME: 5 minutes
COOK TIME: 15 minutes
TOTAL TIME: 20 minutes

½ **pound ground beef**

2 tablespoons soy sauce

1 tablespoon sesame oil

**1 tablespoon light brown
sugar or granulated sugar**

1 tablespoon olive oil

2 garlic cloves, minced

**1 teaspoon minced
fresh ginger**

**Steamed rice or
lettuce leaves**

**Chopped scallions or
sesame seeds, for garnish
(optional)**

This is a modified version of a traditional beef bowl
made with thin slices of beef sirloin. Using ground beef
is a budget-friendly option, and it requires less time
for marinating. Serve over steamed rice or in lettuce
leaves as a wrap.

1. In a large bowl, mix together the ground beef, soy
    sauce, sesame oil, and brown sugar. Set aside to
    marinate for 10 minutes.

2. In a pan, heat the olive oil over medium-low heat.
    Add the garlic and ginger and sauté for 30 seconds.

3. Add the ground beef and cook, stirring with a
    wooden spoon to break up the meat, for about
    5 minutes, or until browned.

4. Serve in a bowl over steamed rice or in let-
    tuce leaves. If desired, garnish with scallions or
    sesame seeds.

REMIX TIP: Top the meat mixture with fresh vegetables
such as sliced cucumbers or grated carrots. You can also
sauté vegetables, such as mushrooms or spinach, and
add them to the bowl just before serving.

Chili Mac and Cheese

20-MINUTE MEAL · ONE AND DONE

SERVES 2

PREP TIME: 10 minutes

COOK TIME: 10 minutes

TOTAL TIME: 20 minutes

½ pound ground beef

½ onion, diced

2 garlic cloves, minced

1 tablespoon chili powder

Pinch salt, plus more to taste

Pinch ground black pepper, plus more to taste

1 (8-ounce) can tomato sauce

1½ cups beef broth

1 cup elbow macaroni

½ cup shredded cheese of choice

Combining two classic comfort foods is a no-brainer, and this dish tastes even better on the second day. The chili is bean-free, but you can add a can of drained and rinsed black or pinto beans. For a creamier option, substitute cream cheese for the shredded cheese, and for a kick, add a diced jalapeño.

1. Heat a pan over medium-high heat. Add the ground beef, onion, garlic, chili powder, salt, and pepper and cook for about 3 minutes, or until the beef is no longer pink.

2. Stir in the tomato sauce, broth, and macaroni. Cover with a lid or aluminum foil, reduce the heat to low, and cook, stirring often to prevent the pasta from sticking, for about 6 minutes, or until the pasta is cooked.

3. Turn off the heat and stir in the cheese. Taste and adjust the seasonings, if desired.

4. Spoon into bowls and serve.

SMART SHOPPING: Save money and buy 2 pounds of ground beef. Divide into four equal portions and store each in a zip-top plastic bag in the fridge to use by the date listed on the package, or freeze them for up to 3 months.

Cheesy Beef Taco Skillet

SERVES 2

PREP TIME: 10 minutes
COOK TIME: 10 minutes
TOTAL TIME: 20 minutes

½ **pound ground beef**

½ **onion, diced**

2 garlic cloves, minced

**1 (10- or 14.5-ounce) can
diced tomatoes with
green chilies**

1 teaspoon chili powder

1 teaspoon ground cumin

1 teaspoon salt

½ **teaspoon ground
black pepper**

**2 corn tortillas, cut into
strips or wedges**

¾ **cup shredded cheese
of choice**

**Optional toppings: chopped
scallions, sour cream,
diced fresh tomatoes, and
sliced avocado**

If you love tacos, you'll find all your favorite flavors here. To save on prep time, use 1 tablespoon of the spice mix from Taco Tuesday (page 61) and omit the seasonings. This is delicious on its own, but the filling is also great for burrito bowls or wraps.

1. Heat a pan over medium-high heat. Add the ground beef and sauté for about 3 minutes, or until browned and no longer pink. Add the onion and garlic and sauté for 2 minutes.

2. Stir in the tomatoes, chili powder, cumin, salt, and pepper. Reduce the heat to low, cover with a lid or aluminum foil, and simmer for 5 minutes.

3. Turn off the heat. Stir and top with the tortilla strips and cheese. Cover with a lid or aluminum foil and let sit for about 2 minutes to melt the cheese.

4. Divide into bowls, add the toppings (if using), and serve.

REMIX TIP: Up the ante by turning the strips of tortilla into chips. Heat ¼ cup of vegetable or canola oil in a pan over medium-high heat. Test the oil by carefully placing a piece of tortilla in the pan. If it sizzles, the oil is hot enough. Add the rest of the wedges and fry until crisp. Transfer to a paper towel–lined plate and sprinkle with salt.

Mongolian Beef Stir-Fry

20-MINUTE MEAL · ONE AND DONE

SERVES 2

PREP TIME: 10 minutes

COOK TIME: 10 minutes

TOTAL TIME: 20 minutes

1 tablespoon olive oil

½ pound ground beef

2 garlic cloves, minced

1 teaspoon minced
   fresh ginger

½ teaspoon red
   pepper flakes

1 tablespoon soy sauce

1 tablespoon hoisin sauce

1 tablespoon rice vinegar

1 tablespoon water

1 tablespoon light
   brown sugar

1 tablespoon cornstarch

Sliced scallions or sesame
   seeds, for garnish
   (optional)

Instead of flank steak, which can be expensive and hard to find, ground beef is used here for a budget-friendlier option. Plus, with a faster cooking time, this at-home take-out favorite is a win-win.

1. In a pan, heat the oil over medium heat. Add the ground beef, garlic, ginger, and pepper flakes and sauté for 3 minutes, breaking up the meat with a spoon.

2. In a small bowl, mix together the soy sauce, hoisin, rice vinegar, water, brown sugar, and cornstarch. Add the sauce to the pan and cook for about 5 minutes, or until the sauce has slightly thickened.

3. Divide into bowls. If desired, garnish with scallions or sesame seeds. Serve hot.

SUBSTITUTION: If you really want to use flank steak instead of ground beef (it will be delicious), cut ½ pound of steak into thin strips against the grain. Toss the meat with 2 tablespoons of cornstarch and cook the meat as directed.

Easy Lasagna

ONE AND DONE

SERVES 2 TO 3

PREP TIME: 10 minutes
COOK TIME: 20 minutes
TOTAL TIME: 30 minutes

1 tablespoon olive oil

½ pound ground beef or bulk sausage

½ onion, diced

2 garlic cloves, minced

1 teaspoon salt

½ teaspoon ground black pepper

1 teaspoon Italian seasoning or dried oregano

½ teaspoon red pepper flakes (optional)

4 lasagna noodles

1 (28-ounce) can crushed tomatoes

2 cups water, plus more if needed

½ cup ricotta cheese

This simple lasagna has all of the comforting flavors of the original but without all of the layering work. Lasagna noodles are preferred here, but you can also use any pasta you have available. If you're not a fan of ricotta cheese, feel free to omit it and replace it with more mozzarella.

1. In a pan, heat the oil over medium heat. Add the ground beef, onion, and garlic and sauté for 3 to 4 minutes. Add the salt, black pepper, Italian seasoning, and red pepper flakes (if using) and stir until combined.

2. Break the lasagna noodles into small pieces and evenly layer the noodles on top of the meat mixture. Pour in the crushed tomatoes and 2 cups water and stir until combined.

3. Cover with a lid or aluminum foil and bring to a simmer. Reduce the heat to low and cook, stirring often, for about 15 minutes, or until the noodles are cooked. If the pasta is still firm after 15 minutes and the liquid has evaporated, add 2 to 3 tablespoons of water and continue to cook for a few minutes, until the pasta is tender.

½ cup shredded
mozzarella cheese

½ cup grated
Parmesan cheese

Chopped fresh basil or
parsley, for garnish
(optional)

4. Turn off the heat. Drop small scoops of ricotta cheese over the noodles and top with mozzarella and Parmesan. Cover with a lid or aluminum foil and let sit for about 3 minutes to melt the cheese.

5. Spoon into bowls and garnish with basil (if using). Serve warm.

COOKING TIP: To reduce the cooking time, use 8 ounces of smaller pasta such as penne or rotini instead of lasagna noodles. In step 3, cook for about 8 minutes instead of 15 minutes.

Chili-Lime Fajita Salad

HEALTHY · ONE AND DONE

SERVES 2
PREP TIME: 20 minutes
COOK TIME: 15 minutes
TOTAL TIME: 35 minutes

FOR THE DRESSING

3 tablespoons olive oil

2 garlic cloves, minced

Juice of 1 lime

1 teaspoon chili powder

1 teaspoon ground cumin

Pinch salt

Pinch ground black pepper

FOR THE SALAD

½ pound blade, skirt, or
   flank steak, cut into slices
   against the grain

1 romaine heart, chopped

1 tomato, chopped

1 tablespoon olive oil

½ onion, sliced

1 red bell pepper,
   thinly sliced

The chili-lime dressing in this fajita salad is used to marinate the beef and adds a special zingy flavor. It can be made ahead of time and stored in an airtight container in the fridge for up to 5 days. For a creamier dressing, add 2 tablespoons of sour cream or plain yogurt.

TO MAKE THE DRESSING

1. In a small bowl, whisk together the olive oil, garlic, lime juice, chili powder, cumin, salt, and pepper.

TO MAKE THE SALAD

2. In a large zip-top plastic bag, combine the sliced steak and half of the dressing, seal, and toss until evenly coated. Let sit to marinate for 15 minutes.

3. In a large bowl, toss together the romaine lettuce and tomato. Set aside.

4. In a pan, heat the oil over medium heat. Add the onion, bell pepper, salt, and pepper and sauté for 3 to 4 minutes. Transfer to the bowl with the romaine and tomato.

1 teaspoon salt

½ teaspoon ground
black pepper

Optional toppings: sliced
avocado, sour cream, and
chopped fresh cilantro

5. Add the beef to the pan and sauté for 3 to
4 minutes, until the beef is cooked through. Transfer to the bowl with the lettuce. Add the remaining
dressing, any optional toppings, and toss together
until well combined.

6. Transfer to plates and serve immediately.

SMART SHOPPING: Check your local grocery website for
weekly specials on meats, which are often on sale for
50 percent off or "buy one, get one free." Also, check the
meat section at the store for other discounts—meats
within a day or two of their sell-by date are often sold at a
reduced price.

Beef Stroganoff

20-MINUTE MEAL · ONE AND DONE

SERVES 2 OR 3

PREP TIME: 5 minutes

COOK TIME: 15 minutes

TOTAL TIME: 20 minutes

1 tablespoon olive oil

½ pound ground beef

½ onion, diced

2 garlic cloves, minced

1 cup sliced mushrooms

1 teaspoon salt, plus more to taste

½ teaspoon ground black pepper, plus more to taste

½ teaspoon garlic powder

2 cups beef broth

1½ cups small pasta shapes, such as rotini or macaroni

¼ cup sour cream or plain yogurt

Beef stroganoff is usually made with high-quality (and expensive) beef cuts like sirloin or rib eye, which are simmered in a mushroom and cream sauce and served over egg noodles. For this simplified version, ground beef and smaller pasta shapes are used for a faster cooking time without losing all the wonderful flavors.

1. In a pan, heat the oil over medium-high heat. Add the ground beef, onion, and garlic and sauté for 3 minutes. Carefully drain any excess fat into a glass jar, ceramic bowl, or metal can. (Discard the fat after it cools—do not pour it down the drain.)

2. Add the mushrooms, salt, pepper, and garlic powder and sauté for 1 minute.

3. Stir in the broth and pasta. Cover with a lid or aluminum foil and bring to a boil. Reduce the heat to medium-low and cook, stirring occasionally, for 6 minutes.

4. Stir in the sour cream and cook uncovered for about 1 minute, or until the pasta is cooked through. Taste and add more seasoning, if desired. The liquid will thicken as it cools.

5. Spoon into bowls and serve warm.

SUBSTITUTION: To make the recipe with rice instead of pasta, add 1 cup of uncooked rice when you add the broth and cook for 15 minutes, or until the rice is tender. To cook without pasta or rice, omit step 3. Add the sour cream, simmer for a few minutes, and serve over mashed or boiled potatoes.

SKILLET
CHOCOLATE
CHIP COOKIES
page 120

CHAPTER 8

Desserts

· · · · · · · · · · · · · · · · ·

Bananas Foster

SERVES 1

PREP TIME: 5 minutes

COOK TIME: 5 minutes

TOTAL TIME: 10 minutes

2 tablespoons unsalted butter or vegan butter

2 tablespoons light brown sugar

Pinch ground cinnamon

1 large or 2 small bananas, halved crosswise, then lengthwise

¼ cup chopped walnuts or pecans (optional)

1 cup vanilla ice cream, for serving

Bananas Foster is a popular dessert from New Orleans in which bananas are flambéed with rum and banana liqueur and then served with vanilla ice cream. This is a simplified version without the flames (in case you don't have a fire extinguisher handy). And if you prefer not to serve it with ice cream, it will still be delicious.

1. In a pan, combine the butter, brown sugar, and cinnamon and cook over medium heat, stirring often, until the butter is melted.

2. Add the bananas and nuts (if using) and cook, stirring often, for 3 to 4 minutes, until the bananas have softened.

3. Spoon into a bowl and serve warm with ice cream.

REMIX TIP: This can be served over pancakes or oatmeal for breakfast. Cut the banana crosswise into slices and cook as directed.

Chocolaty Crispy Rice Bites

MAKES 12 TO 14 BITES
PREP TIME: 25 minutes
COOK TIME: 5 minutes
TOTAL TIME: 30 minutes

2 tablespoons unsalted butter, vegan butter, or coconut oil

2 tablespoons almond butter or another nut butter

2 tablespoons honey

¾ cup chocolate chips or chopped bittersweet chocolate

2 cups crispy rice cereal

Here is a remix of an iconic childhood favorite treat. This version uses nut butter and honey to bind the cereal instead of the traditional marshmallows. Use any brand of crispy rice cereal. These bites can be stored in a covered container for up to 1 week in the fridge.

1. Line a plate with parchment paper or wax paper.
2. In a pan, heat the butter, almond butter, and honey over medium-low heat and mix until smooth, about 1 minute.
3. Stir in the chocolate and cook over medium-low heat, stirring often, until the chocolate has melted.
4. Turn off the heat. Add the rice cereal and stir until well combined.
5. Using a spoon, scoop bite-size portions onto the lined plate. Refrigerate for 20 to 25 minutes to set.

REMIX TIP: Put a little more crunch in these bites by adding 2 tablespoons of chopped nuts, or add unsweetened coconut flakes along with the cereal. Or you can omit the chocolate and, if you prefer, add peanut butter chips or white chocolate.

Crepes

SERVES 2

PREP TIME: 5 minutes

COOK TIME: 15 minutes

TOTAL TIME: 20 minutes

3 tablespoons unsalted
butter, plus more
for cooking

¼ cup milk

¼ cup water

1 large egg

1 tablespoon sugar

1 teaspoon vanilla extract

½ cup all-purpose flour

Pinch salt

Optional toppings: sugar,
honey, whipped cream,
and sliced fruit

Crepes are like thin pancakes that get rolled up and
served with fillings and toppings. Letting the batter
rest helps hydrate the flour and infuse it with the liquid,
resulting in a lighter, fluffier texture. To save time, you
can also chill the batter overnight in the fridge to cook
the next day.

1. In a pan, melt 3 tablespoons of butter over medium
   heat. Turn off the heat and transfer the butter
   to a bowl.

2. Add the milk, water, egg, sugar, and vanilla to the
   bowl with the melted butter and whisk together.
   Add the flour and salt and whisk until just combined. Let the batter rest for about 10 minutes, or
   overnight in the fridge.

3. Heat the pan over medium heat. (If the batter
   rested overnight, add 1 tablespoon butter to the
   pan, otherwise there should still be butter in the
   skillet.) Pour half of the batter into the pan. Pick
   up the pan and swirl it around in a circular motion
   to evenly spread out the batter. Cook for about
   1 minute, until lightly golden on the bottom.

4. Gently slide a spatula under the crepe, flip it over, and cook for about 1 minute, or until lightly golden on the other side. Transfer the crepe to a plate.

5. Add 1 teaspoon of butter to the pan and let melt. Add the remaining batter to the pan and cook like the first one.

6. Roll up the crepes and place one on each of two plates. Add toppings (if using) and serve.

REMIX TIP: For a savory crepe, omit the vanilla and cook as directed. Fill the crepes with deli meats, shredded cheese, or sautéed vegetables, such as spinach or sliced mushrooms.

Skillet Chocolate Chip Cookies

VEGETARIAN

MAKES 12 COOKIES
PREP TIME: 5 minutes
COOK TIME: 45 minutes
TOTAL TIME: 50 minutes

4 tablespoons (½ stick) unsalted butter

¼ cup granulated sugar

¼ cup packed light brown sugar

1 large egg, at room temperature

1 teaspoon vanilla extract

1 cup all-purpose flour

½ teaspoon baking soda

¼ teaspoon salt

½ cup semisweet chocolate chips

Butter or cooking spray for the pan

Who knew you could make cookies in a pan? This method is ideal when you are having a sweet craving and need warm cookies right away. You can just cook a few cookies at a time as the dough can be made ahead, wrapped in plastic wrap, and kept in the fridge for up to 5 days. One batch takes 15 minutes to cook, so you can be eating cookies while you are cooking the rest of the recipe.

1. In a pan, melt the butter over medium heat and transfer to a bowl.

2. Add the granulated sugar and brown sugar to the bowl and whisk together. Add the egg and vanilla and whisk until combined.

3. Add the flour, baking soda, salt, and chocolate chips and, using a rubber spatula, gently mix until just combined.

4. Using a spoon, scoop out four small portions of dough and roll into 1-inch balls. Place them in the pan about 1 inch apart and gently flatten them using the back of a spoon or your fingers.

5. Cover with a lid or aluminum foil and cook on the lowest heat for 15 minutes, or until they look set and golden. (The low heat keeps the cookies from burning, while the cover holds in the heat so they will "bake.")

6. While the first batch is cooking, shape the remaining dough into eight balls, place on a plate, and store in the fridge to chill.

7. When the first batch is done, transfer to a plate. The dough might look soft, but it will firm up as it cools.

8. Add butter or cooking spray to the pan and repeat with the remaining batches.

9. Eat warm. Store in a covered container for up to 3 days.

REMIX TIP: Replace the chocolate chips with white chocolate chips, M&M's, or Reese's Pieces. You can also add 2 tablespoons of chopped nuts, rolled oats, or almond butter for different flavors and textures.

Skillet Brownies

20-MINUTE MEAL · VEGETARIAN

SERVES 4

PREP TIME: 5 minutes
COOK TIME: 15 minutes
TOTAL TIME: 20 minutes

4 tablespoons (½ stick) unsalted butter

¾ cup semisweet chocolate chips, divided

¼ cup unsweetened cocoa powder or chopped bittersweet chocolate

1 large egg, at room temperature

1 teaspoon vanilla extract

¼ cup packed light brown sugar

¼ cup all-purpose flour

¼ teaspoon baking soda

¼ teaspoon salt

COOKING TIP: Overmixing will result in dry and dense brownies, so be careful and stir until just combined.

If you're a chocolate lover, you'll adore these rich and decadent brownies. The ingredients are similar to the chocolate chip cookie recipe on page 120 but with different measurement ratios and the addition of cocoa powder. Devour the warm brownies as is or with a scoop of ice cream on the side.

1. In a pan, combine the butter, ½ cup of chocolate chips, and cocoa powder and warm over low heat until melted. Turn off the heat.

2. In a small bowl, whisk together the egg, vanilla, and brown sugar until combined. Add the mixture to the pan and stir. Add the flour, baking soda, salt, and the remaining ¼ cup of chocolate chips. Using a rubber spatula, mix gently until just combined. Use the spatula to smooth out the batter.

3. Cover with a lid or aluminum foil and cook on the lowest heat setting for 8 to 10 minutes, until the top is set. The brownies might seem too soft, but they will continue to cook as they sit. Turn off the heat and let cool for a few minutes.

4. Cut and serve warm.

Fruit Crisp

SERVES 2

PREP TIME: 5 minutes

COOK TIME: 10 minutes

TOTAL TIME: 15 minutes

FOR THE CRISP

2 tablespoons unsalted butter or vegan butter

2 tablespoons light brown sugar or other sweetener

1 teaspoon vanilla extract

Pinch ground cinnamon

Pinch salt

1/2 cup old-fashioned rolled oats

FOR THE FRUIT

1 tablespoon unsalted butter or vegan butter

1 tablespoon light brown sugar or other sweetener

Pinch ground cinnamon

2 apples, pears, or peaches, peeled, cored or pitted, and cut into bite-size pieces

This is a deconstructed version of pie without all the work. The fruit is cooked with butter and sugar and topped with a crunchy oat topping.

TO MAKE THE CRISP

1. In a pan, combine the butter, brown sugar, vanilla, cinnamon, and salt and cook over medium heat until the butter has melted. Stir in the oats and cook, stirring often, for about 3 minutes, until lightly browned. Transfer to a plate and set aside.

TO MAKE THE FRUIT

2. Add the butter, brown sugar, and cinnamon to the pan and cook until the butter has melted. Stir in the fruit and cook over medium heat, stirring often, for about 5 minutes, or until tender.

3. Transfer the fruit to a serving bowl, top with the oat mixture, and serve warm.

SMART SHOPPING: Use in-season fruit because it will be less expensive and taste sweeter. To save money, look for fruit on sale. Try using fresh berries, such as strawberries, blueberries, or raspberries.

Vanilla Pudding with Berry Jam

SERVES 1

PREP TIME: 10 minutes, plus 1 hour to chill

COOK TIME: 10 minutes

TOTAL TIME: 1 hour 20 minutes

1 cup milk

3 tablespoons sugar

1 tablespoon cornstarch

Pinch salt

1 teaspoon vanilla extract

1 tablespoon unsalted butter

2 tablespoons Berry Jam (page 55) or ¼ cup fresh berries, for serving

REMIX TIP: To make chocolate pudding, add 1½ tablespoons of unsweetened cocoa powder along with the milk and continue with the recipe as instructed.

Homemade pudding is silky and creamy, and this one is no exception. The cornstarch helps thicken the pudding, which will set when chilled. The pudding can be made in advance, stored in an airtight container, and refrigerated for up to 5 days.

1. In a pan, heat the milk over medium heat until it starts to bubble.

2. In a small bowl, mix together the sugar, cornstarch, and salt.

3. Slowly pour the sugar mixture into the pan, whisking constantly. Reduce the heat to low and continue to cook, stirring constantly, for a few minutes, or until it thickens.

4. Turn off the heat and stir in the vanilla and butter. Transfer the mixture to a bowl and let cool.

5. Place a piece of plastic wrap directly on the surface of the pudding to avoid a skin forming and refrigerate for about 1 hour. The pudding will continue to thicken as it chills.

6. To serve, stir in the berry jam or top with fresh berries.

Easy Poached Pears

5 OR FEWER INGREDIENTS · 20-MINUTE MEAL · ONE AND DONE · VEGAN

SERVES 2 TO 4

PREP TIME: 5 minutes

COOK TIME: 15 minutes

TOTAL TIME: 20 minutes

2 cups water

½ cup sugar

1 teaspoon vanilla extract

½ lemon, sliced

2 Bosc or Anjou pears, peeled, cored, and quartered

Optional toppings: whipped cream, ice cream, or mascarpone

SMART SHOPPING: Don't choose overripe pears or soft pear varieties like Bartlett or Comice. Those will get too mushy during cooking. Firmer varieties, such as Bosc and Anjou, are the best options for this recipe.

Poached pears may sound fancy or difficult to make, but they are actually super easy. You can customize the poaching liquid by adding a cinnamon stick or a slice of fresh ginger. This dessert can be made ahead, stored in an airtight container, and refrigerated for up to 5 days. When ready to serve, reheat the pears in the poaching liquid until warmed through. Other fruits you can use are apples, apricots, peaches, and plums. Poached fruit can be served on its own or with a topping if you want an impressive dessert for guests.

1. In a pan, heat the water, sugar, vanilla, and lemon over medium heat, stirring often, until the sugar is fully dissolved.

2. Reduce the heat to low, add the pears, and simmer for about 10 minutes, turning the pears over often, until they are cooked through. (If making ahead, let the pears cool and store in the poaching liquid.)

3. Remove the pears from the poaching liquid with a slotted spoon and serve plain or with any of the toppings.

MEASUREMENT CONVERSIONS

VOLUME EQUIVALENTS

	U.S. STANDARD	U.S. STANDARD (OUNCES)	METRIC (APPROXIMATE)
LIQUID	2 tablespoons	1 fl. oz.	30 mL
	¼ cup	2 fl. oz.	60 mL
	½ cup	4 fl. oz.	120 mL
	1 cup	8 fl. oz.	240 mL
	1½ cups	12 fl. oz.	355 mL
	2 cups or 1 pint	16 fl. oz.	475 mL
	4 cups or 1 quart	32 fl. oz.	1 L
	1 gallon	128 fl. oz.	4 L
DRY	⅛ teaspoon	—	0.5 mL
	¼ teaspoon	—	1 mL
	½ teaspoon	—	2 mL
	¾ teaspoon	—	4 mL
	1 teaspoon	—	5 mL
	1 tablespoon	—	15 mL
	¼ cup	—	59 mL
	⅓ cup	—	79 mL
	½ cup	—	118 mL
	⅔ cup	—	156 mL
	¾ cup	—	177 mL
	1 cup	—	235 mL
	2 cups or 1 pint	—	475 mL
	3 cups	—	700 mL
	4 cups or 1 quart	—	1 L
	½ gallon	—	2 L
	1 gallon	—	4 L

CONTINUED >>

OVEN TEMPERATURES

FAHRENHEIT	CELSIUS (APPROXIMATE)
250°F	120°C
300°F	150°C
325°F	165°C
350°F	180°C
375°F	190°C
400°F	200°C
425°F	220°C
450°F	230°C

WEIGHT EQUIVALENTS

U.S. STANDARD	METRIC (APPROXIMATE)
½ ounce	15 g
1 ounce	30 g
2 ounces	60 g
4 ounces	115 g
8 ounces	225 g
12 ounces	340 g
16 ounces or 1 pound	455 g

RESOURCES

SHOPPING

Amazon has a wide selection of pans and skillets available to choose from for any budget. They also carry every kitchen utensil or piece of cooking equipment you might need. **(Amazon.com)**

Target offers many types of pans and kitchen utensils to choose from. You can also shop at Target for all your groceries as well. **(Target.com)**

Walmart also offers various types of pans to choose from both in store and online. In addition to kitchen equipment, you can also buy groceries at very reasonable prices. **(Walmart.com)**

COOKBOOKS

Ellgen, Pamela. *The 5-Ingredient College Cookbook: Easy, Healthy Recipes for the Next Four Years & Beyond*. Rockridge Press, 2017.
This book has 100 simple, easy-to-follow recipes. Perfect for beginner cooks, the recipes are done in 30 minutes with only 5 ingredients.

Hu, Emily, PhD. *College Cooking for One: 75 Easy, Perfectly Portioned Recipes for Student Life*. Rockridge Press, 2020.
In addition to offering healthy and budget-friendly recipes for one, this book also explains how to adapt recipes for vegetarian and vegan diets.

INDEX

INDEX

INDEX

INDEX

INDEX

INDEX

INDEX

INDEX

INDEX

INDEX

ABOUT THE AUTHOR

MJ Hong is a recipe developer and cooking instructor who has taught more than 10,000 students how to cook international cuisines. She left her corporate executive position in 2010 to pursue her passion for food, wine, and entertaining and has owned a private event venue and winery for 10 years.

She currently teaches in-person and virtual cooking classes, food and wine pairing classes, and culinary team-building challenges for companies. Her goal is to travel the world to expand her culinary knowledge and continue teaching as she travels.

MJ lives in California, and nothing makes her happier than cooking and testing recipes with her granddaughter. You can visit her website at CulinaryAdventureswithMJ.com.

CPSIA information can be obtained
at www.ICGtesting.com
Printed in the USA
JSHW040147281121
20777JS00005B/7